The New Yiddish Kitchen

The New Yiddish Kitchen

Gluten-Free and Paleo Kosher Recipes for the Holidays and Every Day

Simone Miller
bestselling author of *The Zenbelly Cookbook*

Jennifer Robins
bestselling author of *Down South Paleo*

PAGE STREET
PUBLISHING CO.

PAGE STREET
PUBLISHING CO.

First published in 2016 by

Page Street Publishing Co.

27 Congress Street, Suite 103

Salem, MA 01970

www.pagestreetpublishing.com

Distributed by Macmillan, sales in Canada by The Canadian Manda Group.

19   18   17   16   1   2   3   4   5

ISBN-13: 9781624142307

ISBN-10: 1624142303

Library of Congress Control Number: 2015946805

Cover and book design by Page Street Publishing Co.

Photography by Simone Miller and Jennifer Robins

Printed and bound in China

Page Street is proud to be a member of 1% for the Planet. Members donate one percent of their sales to one or more of the over 1,500 environmental and sustainability charities across the globe who participate in this program.

To bubbes everwhere, past, present and future.
May your traditions continue to be passed down for generations to come.

 **Mollie**–Jennifer's maternal great-grandmother—was under 5 feet tall but sure made up for it with her lively personality. While born in Galveston, Texas, her parents immigrated from Eastern Europe and thus began the multiple generations of Jennifer's Texas-born Jewish family!

 **Jennie**–Jennifer's maternal grandmother (and daughter of Mollie), who was the eldest of 4 daughters. She would tell you stories of making biscuits on Saturday mornings, her "job" as the oldest child. Later, Jennie created many more memories in the kitchen, especially on Passover, when extended family would gather around her dining room table with her piping hot matzo ball soup.

 **Rose**–Simone's paternal great-grandmother—came from a family of thirteen Russian immigrants. Although she had no formal education, she was amazingly intuitive, hilarious and one of the world's greatest storytellers. Her Bronx, NY, apartment was always filled with aromas of chickens roasting and challah baking.

 **Helen**–Simone's maternal grandmother—grew up in Poland with 6 brothers and sisters. She emigrated to the U.S. 8 years after surviving the Holocaust, eager to begin a new life with her new family. Nothing makes her happier than holiday dinners surrounded by loved ones. At 97, she remains a positive, nurturing, loving source of inspiration.

Contents

Not-So-Traditional Deli Fare • 67

Pastured Meats and Main Courses • 111

Dairy-Free Condiments and Sauces • 213

Holiday Menus and Tips • 237

Introduction

The New Yiddish Kitchen is a labor of love born from complete desperation. *All right*, that's a little dramatic. But when we began our search for grain-free Jewish recipes for the holidays (*and every day*), we came up pretty short-handed. Sure there were Thanksgiving, Christmas, Halloween and Easter recipes galore … but what about a grain-free challah for goodness sakes?! What about those traditional Jewish deli favorites? Where are the grain- and gluten-free counterparts for matzo ball soup, we ask?!

Jewish inspired foods are staples to many "Yiddish kitchens" around the globe. They fill the bellies and hearts of the masses, many of whom aren't even Jewish. But when you take away gluten, grain and dairy, those favorite Jewish foods are few and far between, to be honest. We love our baked goods and cream cheese, but without grain or dairy, celebrating with these foods gets a little complicated.

Once we started brainstorming, we became passionately inspired to re-create some childhood (and adulthood) favorites. We wanted to take the traditional holiday delights, as well as everyday Jewish staples, and make them edible again for those with food restrictions like ours. All the recipes in this book are *entirely* grain- and gluten-free and provide alternatives to dairy in the rare times they are used. For those cooking from a religious perspective, this book was also written with kosher laws in mind, meaning that most kosher laws should be observed as long as the ingredients you purchase comply.

Our recipes are all also compliant with Paleo and gluten-free lifestyles, as they are entirely whole-foods based and free of grain, gluten, refined sugar and dairy.

In *The New Yiddish Kitchen*, we have put together a menu for each one of the annual Jewish holidays to help you prepare as they approach, including a few Shabbat menus so that you can shake things up and rotate out recipes without the same old "schpread." The recipes here are certainly delicious year round, so if you are craving matzo ball soup in the summer, be sure to make a pot! And quite honestly, when are latkes *ever* a bad idea? *Exactly*. Never.

If you've found yourself searching for gluten- and grain-free Jewish recipes and have come up empty handed, we're here to put an end to your kvetching. Not Jewish? This is nothing to schvitz about, as we wrote *The New Yiddish Kitchen* from a cultural perspective, aiming to deliver all of your favorites, from deli fare to Israeli-inspired dishes.

Lastly, we wrote this book with a lot of heart and spirit. We'd love to see this book passed down through the years (from bubbes to babies), put on display in your family's kitchen and splattered with schmaltz (a true symbol of honor). Our recipes are literally "for life," and our hope is these recipes leave a lasting impression on your hearts while delivering healing foods to your bodies.

L'chaim! Jennifer & Simone

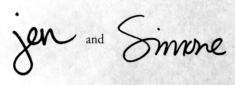

Jen and Simone

A Note About Ingredients

Where is the overlap between Paleo, gluten-free, grass-fed and kosher? They all seem to be such separate entities, if not completely unrelated at times. Gluten-free as a general rule of thumb excludes gluten-containing grains such as wheat, barley and rye. It is the protein in these grains that can cause digestive upset or even systemic inflammation in some people. Paleo takes gluten-free a step further by excluding all grains, plus dairy, legumes, and refined sugar. And unlike gluten-free, the sourcing of the animal protein becomes much more of a focus. So, pasture-raised animals that are treated humanely and fed as nature intended are a focal point, in addition to local and organic produce when it is an option. Kosher, on the other hand, comes from the Jewish laws in which meats and other cooking ingredients must adhere to a specific set of rules in regard to the slaughter and preparation of the aforementioned.

So how do these all fit together? Is it possible to observe both the Paleo lifestyle and kosher laws all at once? It is! It might take a little more research, but it is certainly possible. There are some kosher farms with animals that are also raised humanely and eat "off the land." These are ideal when observing both sets of constructs, but in the end you will want to find the balance and prioritize as you see fit in regard to your body and degree of commitment. With respect to other ingredients you might find in *The New Yiddish Kitchen*, like almond flour, coconut flour, avocado oil, pure maple syrup and others, these are considered Paleo in nature because together they take the place of refined sugars, wheat flour (including whole grain or bleached) and rancid cooking oils. If observing kosher laws as well, there are several online resources to sort out which of these Paleo-approved products are considered kosher. You'll find there are many recipes, which are entirely based upon meat and fresh organic produce. In this case, they are automatically Paleo and gluten-free, and should be kosher as well, given that the meats are protected under kosher law and the produce is fresh (and not processed).

The beauty of eating Paleo is that there are far fewer processed ingredients in general, as the goal is to eat with ancestral intent, so the kosher adaptability should translate relatively simply. Our hope is that those with food intolerances, autoimmune diseases or chronic inflammation will be able to honor their bodies, their eating rituals and their culinary Jewish cravings with the recipes we have written here in *The New Yiddish Kitchen*.

Not-Your-Bubbe's Appetizers and Soups

If you've ever attended or hosted a Passover Seder, you know the beginning of the meal is just as important as, if not more than, the main course. For this reason, I have given equal weight to this chapter where you will find delicious options like Roasted Squash Hummus (page 19), Baba Ghanoush (page 16) and Dill-Pickle Deviled Eggs (page 15) to start your meal. What, you want liver instead?! Of course it's in there. Just as important, homemade chicken soup is the backbone to every Jewish soup recipe. I've created three versions of grain-free Matzo Balls, plus a recipe for Kreplach so that you can build the perfect Jewish Penicillin, on holidays and every day. You can thank me the next time your headache is caused by more than hearing me kvetch!!

Dill-Pickle Deviled Eggs

Deviled eggs are always a crowd favorite, and adding kosher pickles gives them a nice zing.
Make sure you mince the pickles as small as possible to avoid clogging the pastry bag.

Prep Time: 10 minutes Cook Time: 12 minutes Makes: 4–6 servings as an appetizer

Water for steaming

6 eggs

½ cup (120 g) minced kosher pickle (about one large pickle)

¼ cup (65 ml) Mayonnaise (page 228)

1 tablespoon (15 ml) Dijon mustard

1 tablespoon (15 g) minced fresh dill, plus more for garnish

⅛ teaspoon salt

In a pot that fits a steamer basket, bring a small amount of water to a boil. Put the eggs in the steamer basket and place in the pot. Cover, and allow to steam for 12 minutes.

After 12 minutes, carefully remove the basket and dunk the eggs into cold water to cool. Gently crack the eggs all over and then peel. Slice the eggs in half and pop out the yolks.

In the bowl of a food processor, combine the egg yolks, minced pickles, mayonnaise, Dijon mustard, dill and salt. Pulse the ingredients several times to puree.

Scoop the yolk mixture out and fill the egg whites, either with a spoon or pastry bag. Garnish the eggs with additional dill, if desired.

Bubbe's tip: Passover guests too hotsy totsy for plain, hard-boiled eggs? Serve these instead!

Baba Ghanoush

Baba Ghanoush doesn't get nearly as much love as its better-known cousin, hummus, but it should! It's rich and smoky and the perfect addition to your Middle Eastern appetizer platter.

Prep Time: 10 minutes Cook Time: 30 minutes, plus time to cool Makes: 2 cups (475 ml)

1 large eggplant, about 1 pound (450 g)

1 clove garlic, minced

3 tablespoons (45 ml) tahini

3 tablespoons (45 ml) lemon juice

½ teaspoon liquid smoke

1 teaspoon salt

¼ teaspoon paprika, plus more for garnish

1 tablespoon (15 ml) extra virgin olive oil, plus more for garnish

Preheat the oven to 450°F (230°C) and prick the eggplant all over with a fork. Place the eggplant on a baking sheet.

Place the eggplant in the oven and roast for 30 minutes, or until the outside of the eggplant is very soft. Remove from the oven, and allow it to cool for 10 minutes.

Once cool enough to handle, remove the skin from the eggplant. If it's difficult to separate, cut in half or quarters and use a sharp knife to remove it.

In the bowl of a food processor, place the eggplant, garlic, tahini, lemon juice, liquid smoke, salt and paprika. Blend the ingredients until smooth, and then drizzle the olive oil in through the spout.

To serve, drizzle with a little extra virgin olive oil and sprinkle with paprika.

Bubbe's tip: Don't want to use the liquid smoke? Don't get meshuga about it. Use smoked paprika in place of the regular paprika in the recipe. Was that so difficult?

Roasted Squash Hummus

Hummus is off the table when you remove legumes from your diet, which is a shame because almost everyone loves it! Well, there's good news. Roasted squash stands in quite nicely for garbanzos, and you might just find yourself preferring this version to the traditional.

Prep Time: 15 minutes **Cook Time:** 25 minutes **Makes:** About 4 cups (950 ml)

1 medium butternut squash (about 1½ pounds [675 g]), peeled and cut into 1-inch (2.5-cm) pieces

8–10 cloves garlic, peeled

2 tablespoons (30 ml) avocado oil or coconut oil

1 cup (240 ml) tahini

⅓ cup (80 ml) lemon juice

¾ teaspoon salt

¼ cup (60 ml) extra virgin olive oil, plus more for garnish

1 tablespoon (2 g) parsley, minced (optional)

Preheat your oven to 425°F (218°C). Toss the squash and garlic with the avocado oil and spread on a baking sheet.

Roast them for 25 minutes, or until very soft.

Transfer the squash and garlic to the bowl of a food processor and add the tahini, lemon juice and salt. With the motor running, drizzle in the olive oil.

To serve, drizzle with extra virgin olive oil and sprinkle with parsley, if desired.

Bubbe's tip: You kids have everything so easy these days. If you're pressed for time, buy the squash that's already peeled and diced in the supermarket. It will cost you more gelt, but you'll save time, bubula!

Chopped Liver

Chopped liver is a classic Jewish spread that packs in all the health benefits of organ meats while still delivering a delectable dish. Schmaltz, like other animal fats, has gotten a bad rap over the years. But if the fat is rendered from properly raised chickens, it's actually quite a healthy choice.

Prep Time: 10 minutes Cook Time: 12 minutes Makes: 2 cups (475 ml)

3 tablespoons (45 ml) Schmaltz, divided (page 235)

1 pound (450 g) chicken livers, patted dry and trimmed of tough membranes

1 small onion, diced

About 1 teaspoon sea salt

2 hard-boiled eggs, chopped

2 tablespoons (5 g) minced fresh parsley

¼ teaspoon black pepper

In a large skillet, melt 2 tablespoons (30 ml) of the schmaltz over medium high heat. Add the livers and cook for 2 minutes on each side, or until they are just cooked through. Remove them to a bowl.

Add the remaining tablespoon (15 ml) of schmaltz to the skillet and turn the heat down to medium. Add the onions and sauté for 7–8 minutes, or until deep golden brown, stirring often. Add a pinch of salt if they start to brown too much, and turn down the heat a bit.

Once the onions are brown, add the livers back in along with a pinch of salt and cook for 1 minute more.

Transfer the liver and onions, hard-boiled eggs and parsley to the bowl of a food processor and add another pinch of salt and the pepper. Pulse the ingredients 5–6 times, until minced and well incorporated but not completely smooth.

Transfer to a serving dish and chill before serving. Cover tightly with plastic wrap directly on the surface to keep it from drying out.

Serve with matzo (page 44 or 47), crackers (page 43) or your favorite veggies.

Bubbe's tip: What, you're so creative? Then add in your own blend of seasonings, if you wish.

Salmon Gefilte Fish

If there were ever a food that was completely polarizing, it would be gefilte fish.
People either love it or hate it, the latter often being those who haven't tried it until they were adults.
The good news: Making it with fresh salmon and white fish yields a gefilte fish that is nothing
like the kind you're picturing submerged in a jar of fish jelly.

Prep Time: 30 minutes Cook Time: 75–90 minutes Makes: 12–16 servings

FOR THE FISH STOCK

2 pounds (900 g) fish heads,
bones and skin

1 medium onion, peeled and sliced

2 large carrots, roughly chopped

1 teaspoon apple cider vinegar

1 tablespoon (15 g) coconut palm
sugar (optional)

2 teaspoons (10 g) salt

Cold water, just enough to cover
the bones

FOR THE FISH

4 medium carrots

1 small parsnip

1 small onion

2 eggs

⅓ cup (60 g) potato starch

1 teaspoon salt

2 pounds (900 g) salmon, ground
(see note)

1½ pounds (675 g) mild white fish,
such as cod, pike or carp,
ground (see note)

FOR THE FISH STOCK

Place the fish bones, sliced onion, roughly chopped carrots, apple cider vinegar, coconut palm sugar and salt in a medium stockpot. Add cold water to cover and bring to a boil.

Allow the stock to simmer for 50–60 minutes, until the vegetables are very soft. Strain the stock and discard the vegetables and bones. Place the stock in a large, deep sauté pan and set aside.

FOR THE FISH

Grate 2 of the carrots and the parsnip. If you are using a food processor to do this, you may need to switch to the chopping blade after shredding, so the vegetables get very finely minced.

Grate the onion and squeeze out the excess liquid.

In a large bowl, whisk together the eggs, potato starch and salt. Mix in the grated vegetables. Add the fish and mix with your hands until well combined. Form the fish mixture into oval patties about ¼ cup (55 g) each.

Peel and slice the remaining carrots.

Bring the stock back up to a simmer and add the fish patties and sliced carrots. Simmer for 10 minutes, flip the fish and simmer another 5 minutes. Chill the stock, fish and carrots for at least 1 hour, or until very cold. Serve the fish cold with the sliced carrots and a little of the stock, if desired.

Note: If you don't have a meat grinder, ask your fish monger to grind the fish for you.

Bubbe's tip: What, it's too much work for you? In my day, the recipe started with "catch a fish," so quit your kvetching!

Jewish Penicillin: Build Your Perfect Bowl

Building your perfect bowl of Jewish Penicillin doesn't have to be difficult,
all the tools are found right here!

1. Choose your broth—whether you pressure cook or slow cook, your broth is the basis for everything. Pick your option from page 27 or page 28. You'll need around 8 ounces (240 ml) for each bowl.

2. Choose your veggies. Do you prefer lots of carrots? Or maybe just onions and celery? Now is the time to select your preferred vegetables and boil them in the stock until they become nice and tender, or more al dente if you like. You'll want around 2 ounces (56 g) of diced veggies per bowl, or more or less depending on your preference.

3. Choose your "noodle." Care to add in zoodles, squoodles or sweet poodles? (That's sweet potato noodles, not canines!) Add about 2 ounces (56 g) of your favorite noodle per bowl. See options and cooking instructions on page 34.

4. Choose kreplach, matzo balls or both. On pages 29, 30 and 33 you'll find varieties of matzo balls and our grain-free kreplach as well. Find your perfect combination adding those to the mix. Around 3–4 matzo balls or kreplach typically will do the trick for a single bowl; they are starchy and filling! These just need a few minutes in the broth to heat through.

Bubbe's tip: There is no right answer, bubula; it's all about finding your joy. If kreplach makes you plotz and you're sensitive to nightshades, just pick your matzo balls and veggies based on what makes it geshmak. That's what it's all about!

Slow Cooker Chicken Broth

If effortless is your game, this broth has your name written all over it. Toss in the ingredients and let the slow cooker do its job. You'll find this slow cooker chicken broth is rich and flavorful, much more so than store-bought packaged broth. You can also freeze this recipe and pull it out when you want to make a batch of Matzo Ball Soup (page 24, 29 or 30).

Prep Time: 5 minutes Cook Time: 24–36 hours Makes: 12 servings

2–3 pounds (900–1,350 g) chicken bones

1–2 pounds (450–900 g) vegetables (carrots, onions, celery or other desired ones), roughly chopped

2–3 cloves of garlic

1 teaspoon sea salt

Fresh ground pepper to taste

Bay leaves, parsley, dill or any other fresh herbs

3 tablespoons (45 ml) apple cider vinegar

Place the chicken bones in the slow cooker with selected vegetables and garlic and cover with water. Add in seasonings, herbs and apple cider vinegar.

Turn on the slow cooker and cook on low for 24 hours or longer. Strain broth and discard the bones, veggies and meat (if any remains). Refrigerate, freeze or use right away.

Note: Some slow cookers have an automatic turnoff, so check yours to see if it needs to be turned back on or reset.

Note: Prefer beef broth? Simply swap out the bones! Roasting the bones at 425°F (218°C) for 30 minutes will give the broth even more flavor.

Bubbe's tip: The apple cider vinegar helps release the minerals and nutrients from the bones. Don't forget it!

Pressure Cooker Chicken Broth

Chicken broth that simmers all day? There's nothing wrong with that, but if you're pressed for time, this is the broth for you. You'll get a rich, delicious broth in under 2 hours.

Prep Time: 10 minutes Cook Time: 2 hours Makes: About 4 quarts (3.8 L)

4–5 pounds (1.8–2.25 kg) chicken bones (backs, necks, feet and carcasses from roast chickens you've reserved)

1 tablespoon (15 ml) apple cider vinegar

1 teaspoon salt

1 pound (450 g) carrots, halved

1 pound (450 g) parsnips, halved

1 celery root, peeled and quartered

1 onion, quartered

A few cloves garlic, whole and unpeeled

1 bunch parsley or dill

Into the pressure cooker, place the chicken bones, apple cider vinegar and salt. Cover with cold water and lock on the lid.

Once the pot comes up to pressure, turn the heat to the lowest temperature necessary to keep the pressure valve popped. Allow the mixture to cook for 1 hour.

After an hour, turn off the heat and let the pressure release. Once unlocked, remove the lid and add the vegetables and herbs.

Bring back up to a rolling boil and reduce for 1 hour, uncovered, or until the vegetables are very soft.

Strain the broth, reserving the liquid and discarding the bones and vegetables.

Note: Prefer beef broth? Simply swap out the bones! Roasting bones at 425°F (218°C) for 30 minutes will give the broth even more flavor.

Bubbe's tip: Don't have a pressure cooker? Of course you can still have broth! Just follow the instructions in this recipe, increasing the initial cook time to 3–4 hours.

Matzo Balls (Sweet Potato Kneidlach)

Prep Time: 10 minutes Cook Time: 35 minutes Makes: 6–8 servings (about 20 small dumplings)

36 ounces (1 L) water or Chicken Broth (page 27 or 28), for boiling the potatoes and matzo balls

1 pound (450 g) Japanese sweet potato (about 2 medium), peeled and sliced

2 eggs

¼ cup (24 g) potato starch

¼ cup (24 g) tapioca starch

1 tablespoon (15 g) coconut flour

2 tablespoons (30 ml) olive oil, Schmaltz (page 235) or avocado oil

½ teaspoon sea salt

¼ teaspoon garlic powder

¼ teaspoon onion powder

Combine the water or broth and sliced sweet potatoes in a large stock pot and bring to a boil. Cook for 20 minutes, or until tender. Turn off the heat, remove the potatoes and allow them to cool for 10 minutes or so. Reserve the water in the pot—you'll use it to cook the matzo balls.

While the potatoes are cooling, whisk together the eggs, potato starch, tapioca starch, coconut flour, olive oil, salt, garlic powder and onion powder. Once the potatoes have cooled off a bit, mash them into the egg mixture, making sure everything is well incorporated.

Bring the pot of water back up to a simmer. To make the matzo balls, you can either roll them into balls, about a heaping tablespoon each, or you can scoop the dough with a small cookie scoop with a lever.

Drop the matzo balls into the simmering water and cook for 15 minutes. Serve in piping hot chicken soup. See page 24 for our tips on how to build the perfect bowl!

Matzo Balls (Potato Kneidlach)

Prep Time: 10 minutes Cook Time: 35 minutes Makes: 6–8 servings (about 20 small dumplings)

36 ounces (1 L) water or Chicken Broth (page 27 or 28), for boiling the potatoes and matzo balls

1 pound (450 g) Yukon gold or red bliss potatoes (about 2 large), peeled and sliced

2 eggs

½ cup (50 g) potato starch

1 tablespoon (15 ml) olive oil, Schmaltz (page 235) or avocado oil

1 tablespoon (10 g) fresh minced dill (or ½ tablespoon dried)

½ teaspoon sea salt

¼ teaspoon black pepper

¼ teaspoon onion powder

Combine the water or broth and sliced potatoes in a large stock pot and bring to a boil. Cook for 20 minutes, or until tender. Turn off the heat, remove the potatoes and allow them to cool for 10 minutes or so. Reserve the water in the pot—you'll use it to cook the matzo balls.

While the potatoes are cooling, whisk together the eggs, potato starch, olive oil, dill, salt, black pepper and onion powder. Once the potatoes have cooled off a bit, mash them into the egg mixture, making sure everything is well incorporated.

Bring the pot of water back up to a simmer. To make the matzo balls, you can either roll them into balls with your hands, about a heaping tablespoon each, or you can scoop the dough with a small cookie scoop with a lever.

Drop the matzo balls into the simmering water and cook for 15 minutes. Serve in piping hot chicken soup. See page 24 for our tips on how to build the perfect bowl!

Cassava Flour Matzo Balls

This nightshade-, nut-free matzo ball recipe is a hybrid between a "sinker" and a "floater" and is seasoned perfectly with onion, sea salt and garlic. If you are a dill fan, be sure to add in some fresh chopped dill to suit your fancy!

Prep Time: 5 minutes Cook Time: 10 minutes Makes: 4 servings

Water or Chicken Broth (page 27 or 28), for boiling

½ cup (60 g) cassava flour

3 eggs

1 tablespoon (15 ml) Schmaltz (page 235), avocado oil or olive oil

¼ teaspoon sea salt (or more to taste)

¼ teaspoon garlic powder (or more to taste)

¼ teaspoon onion powder (or more to taste)

1 tablespoon (10 g) minced fresh dill, optional

In a large pot, bring the water or broth to a boil over high heat. Mix together the cassava flour, eggs, schmaltz, sea salt, garlic powder, onion powder and dill, if using.

Drop the dough into the water or broth, about 1 tablespoon (15 g) at a time using a small cookie scoop.

Cook over high heat until they float to the surface, about 1 or 2 minutes, and then allow to simmer for another 5 minutes.

Serve in a piping hot chicken soup. See page 24 for our tips on how to build the perfect bowl.

Bubbe's tip: Overcooking these can make them denser and heavier. If you want them to stay a bit fluffy around the outside, keep cook time short and sweet!

Kreplach

Kreplach are small delicious dumplings traditionally filled with meat or cheese and often served in a bowl of piping hot soup. Sometimes they are fried, making them more similar to pierogi. However you cook them, they are typically made using wheat-based flour, making them off limits to many. In this rendition, cassava flour is used, creating a traditional feel with more tolerable, whole-food ingredients!

Prep Time: 30 minutes Cook Time: 30 minutes Makes: 4–6 servings

½ pound (225 g) boneless skinless chicken breast

2 tablespoons (30 ml) olive oil, divided

½ teaspoon onion powder

1 teaspoon garlic sea salt

¼ teaspoon ground black pepper

1 cup (110 g) carrots, diced

1 onion, diced

Fresh minced dill to taste

1½ cups (183 g) cassava flour, plus more if needed

3 eggs

3 tablespoons (45 ml) olive or avocado oil, plus more if needed

1 teaspoon sea salt

36 ounces (1,080 ml) Chicken Broth (page 27 or 28) or water

Bubbe's tip: I want that you should be happy. If chicken does not put a smile on that punim, then by all means stuff these with brisket.

Preheat the oven to 350°F (175°C) and place the chicken in a baking dish with 1 tablespoon (15 ml) of the olive oil, onion powder, garlic salt and black pepper. Bake for 20-25 minutes or until the juices run clear and the center is cooked.

Alternatively you can use a pressure cooker by cooking on high pressure for 15 minutes.

While the chicken is cooking, sauté the carrots and onions in the remaining olive oil in a small skillet over medium-high heat for about 10–12 minutes or until the vegetables have softened.

Once the chicken is cooked, remove it from the oven or pressure cooker. Cut it into smaller chunks and then, in a blender, combine the chicken, cooked onion, carrots and dill. Blend or pulse until the ingredients are well combined and no large chunks are left. You want it thicker than a puree but ground enough to spoon into the center of the kreplach dough.

To make the dough, combine the flour, eggs, oil and salt. Stir in a bowl to combine and then knead by hand. You may find that you need a little more flour if the dough is too wet or a little more oil if it is too dry. Once you have a ball of dough, pinch off about an eighth of the dough and roll it through your pasta maker on the sheets setting. You want to use a thicker setting because this dough is more delicate than traditional wheat based dough and cannot be rolled as thin.

Lightly flour (with cassava flour) the surface where the dough will be rolled out. The dough going through the pasta maker will need to be very well oiled. Once you've rolled it through, handling it very carefully, use a 3- to 4-inch (7.6–10-cm) glass or biscuit cutter to cut circles in the dough. If you do not have a pasta maker, just roll the dough as thin as you can and then cut circles with the glass or biscuit cutter.

Bring your pot of broth or water to a boil over high heat.

Take about a teaspoon (or less) of the filling mixture and place it into the center of each dough circle. Do not overfill. You can either fold the dough circles in half and pinch to seal closed or you can fold them in triangles similarly to the Hamantaschen (page 179). After choosing your desired shape, repeat steps above until all your dough is filled.

Carefully drop the filled dumplings into the boiling broth or water until they float to the top. Then allow them to cook for a few more minutes. Now they are ready to eat as is or can be part of "Jewish Penicillin: Build Your Perfect Bowl" on page 24.

Noodles for Soup

You might think that noodles are off the table (or out of the soup) when you give up grains, but there are options! Vegetables cut with a spiral slicer, a vegetable peeler or julienne peeler make a wonderful noodle stand-in.

Zucchini, summer squash: About ½ pound (225 g) per serving. Cut with a spiral slicer, peeler or julienne peeler. Simmer in broth for 5 minutes, or until soft.

Sweet potato: About ¼ pound (113 g) per serving. Peel and cut with a spiral slicer or julienne peeler. Simmer in broth for 10 minutes, or until soft.

Celery root: About ¼ pound (113 g) per serving. Peel and cut with a spiral slicer or julienne peeler. Simmer in broth for 10 minutes, or until soft.

Parsnips: About ¼ pound (113 g) per serving. Peel and cut with a handheld julienne peeler or vegetable peeler. Simmer in broth for 10 minutes, or until soft.

Carrots: About ¼ pound (113 g) per serving. Cut with a handheld vegetable peeler or julienne peeler. Simmer in broth for 10 minutes, or until soft.

Spaghetti squash: About ¼ pound (113 g) per serving. Cut in half, scoop out seeds and roast in a 400°F (205°C) oven flesh down, with some water under the squash halves for 30–45 minutes, or until soft. Use a fork to remove the squash from the peel.

Borscht

Borscht is as beautiful as it is nutrient dense. Made with deep-red-colored beets and topped with a swirl of dairy-free cream, you will certainly channel your inner bubbe when you make this one.

Prep Time: 5 minutes   **Cook Time:** 45 minutes   **Makes:** 8 servings

3 large red beets, peeled and diced
2 large carrots, diced
1 large onion, diced
2 tablespoons (30 ml) avocado oil
6 cups (2.7 kg) Beef Broth (page 27)
⅓ cup (80 ml) coconut cream
1 tablespoon (7 g) tapioca starch
Sea salt + pepper to taste

In a large stockpot over medium-heat, sauté the beets, carrots and onion for 15 minutes in the avocado oil. Next, add in the beef broth and bring to a simmer. Allow the vegetables to simmer for about 30 minutes, or until tender.

In a large blender puree the soup mixture, doing so in small batches if necessary.

Pour the soup back into the stockpot and turn the heat to low. Introduce the coconut cream and stir well.

In a small bowl or cup, take about a quarter cup (60 ml) of the soup and combine it with the tapioca starch. Mix it well to make a slurry, and then pour it back into the stockpot. Stir well and allow the soup to thicken over the next few minutes.

Add sea salt and pepper to taste and serve hot.

Bubbe's tip: I want that you should make this gorgeous! Just spoon a dollop of dairy-free sour cream or coconut cream for a culinary delight.

Sweet and Sour Cabbage Soup

This soup is the epitome of Eastern European comfort food with its hearty warmth and diverse flavors.
On a chilly night, few things are as satisfying as a big bowl of Sweet and Sour Cabbage Soup.
Serve with a thick slice of Marble Rye (page 51)!

Prep Time: 15 minutes   Cook Time: 90 minutes   Makes: 4–6 servings

1½ pounds (675 g) beef stew meat, or chuck roast cut into 1-inch (2.5-cm) cubes

6 cups (1.4 L) Chicken or Beef Broth (page 27 or 28)

1 medium head cabbage, about 1½ pounds (675 g), diced into 1-inch (2.5-cm) pieces

1 small onion, diced

2 tablespoons (30 ml) olive oil

14 ounces (580 ml) jarred diced tomatoes

2 tablespoons (30 ml) tomato paste

2 tablespoons (30 ml) honey

¼ cup (60 ml) apple cider vinegar

1 teaspoon paprika

1 teaspoon salt

½ teaspoon cayenne

Bring the meat and the broth to a boil in a large pot. Turn the heat down to medium-low so it comes to a simmer. Skim the froth that gathers on the top and cover. Allow it to simmer for 75 minutes, or until tender.

Preheat the oven to 425°F (218°C).

Toss the cabbage and onion with the olive oil and arrange on a baking sheet. Place in the preheated oven and roast for 45 minutes, stirring after 30.

After 75 minutes, remove the beef from the broth with a slotted spoon. Cut and/or shred into smaller pieces. Return back to the broth along with the roasted cabbage and onions, diced tomatoes, tomato paste, honey, vinegar, paprika, salt and cayenne.

Bring the soup to a boil and then turn down to medium and allow it to simmer, uncovered for 15–20 minutes.

Bubbe's tip: Did you recently make enough brisket to kill a horse? If so, you can make a quick version of this soup with that. Just skip the boiling part at the beginning and add the brisket during the last 15–20 minutes.

Grain-Free Breads and Crackers to Make You "Challah"

By now I think we've established our love for all things starch. It's like asking the question, "Why on this night do we recline?" I'm pretty sure it's so you can cram more carby matzo balls in, am I right? Or more Challah on Friday nights. Or more marble rye at the deli. Bread equals comfort, and after all the suffering, we deserve more bread! But when traditional, wheat-based breads can cause our people even more suffering, we need to ask a new question. Why do I torture myself? Oy vey! So for you we wrote this chapter filled with all of your favorites— *five* bagel variations, *two* Matzo recipes, Challah, Bialys, Rye Bread and even Pita Bread. We say kvetch less, enjoy more! And you can quote your bubbe on that one!

Note: You'll notice that for some of these recipes, the primary measurements for certain ingredients are listed in metric weights. This is for greater precision; however, if you don't have a metric scale, traditional U.S. measurements are included for you as well.

Everything Crackers

These have all the flavor of an everything bagel, but in a crispy cracker!
They're great for a nosh and are the perfect thing for serving with Chopped Liver (page 20).

Prep Time: 10 minutes Cook Time: 16–20 minutes Makes: About 50 crackers

1 large egg (more if needed, see Bubbe's tip)

1 tablespoon (15 ml) extra virgin olive oil

¾ cup (84 g) almond flour

½ cup (64 g) arrowroot powder

¼ cup (56 g) assorted seeds, such as sesame, caraway, black caraway, poppy

¼ teaspoon onion flakes

½ teaspoon finely ground sea salt

Preheat the oven to 350°F (177°C).

In a large mixing bowl, beat the egg with the olive oil.

Stir in the almond flour, arrowroot powder, seeds, onion flakes and salt until the dough comes together. Give it a knead or two to make sure it's well incorporated.

Roll out the dough between two sheets of parchment paper to a thickness of about ⅛ inch (3 mm). Try to get it as close to a rectangle as possible. Remove the top sheet of parchment paper.

With a sharp knife, cut the dough into 1-inch (2.5-cm) squares.

Slide the bottom sheet of parchment paper and dough onto a baking sheet and bake for 10–12 minutes or until the crackers begin to brown.

Turn the heat down to 325°F (163°C) and bake for an additional 6–8 minutes, or until the crackers are crisp and light golden brown.

Remove the crackers from the oven and allow them to cool before breaking apart.

Store the crackers in an airtight container.

Bubbe's tip: Is your dough a little crumbly? Don't plotz! Beat another egg and add a little bit at a time until the dough comes together into a kneadable ball.

Matzo

What happens when Passover rolls around and gluten and grain are off the table?
Passover without matzo just isn't Passover!

Prep Time: 35 minutes Cook Time: 40 minutes Makes: 4 servings

3 cups (700 g) peeled, coarsely chopped yuca root

3 tablespoons (45 ml) avocado oil (or preferred cooking fat)

1 teaspoon sea salt

1 tablespoon (7 g) water chestnut flour or coconut flour, if needed

Preheat the oven to 375°F (190°C). Bring 10 cups (2.4 L) of water to a boil in a large stockpot over high heat. Carefully drop in the chopped yuca root and boil for 20–25 minutes or until fork tender. Drain the water and remove the yuca from the stockpot.

Once the yuca is cool enough to handle, remove the woody core from the center of each piece and discard. Then, in a heavy-duty blender or food processor, combine the yuca, oil and sea salt. Blend until a dough is formed, doing so in small batches if necessary. You'll want to remove all lumps, if possible, so that the dough is smooth. If you have a blender with a tamper, using that will help to get the chunks of yuca under the blades more successfully.

Next, spoon the dough onto a piece of parchment paper and allow it to cool slightly. If the dough is sticky after cooling, you may incorporate the coconut or water chestnut flour by hand until the stickiness is gone. Otherwise divide the dough into 4 equal pieces.

Take one piece and roll it out on a piece of parchment paper, using a knife or pizza cutter to make a square shape. You can incorporate the cutoff dough by placing it on top of the rolled out dough and rolling it back into it.

Then, take a fork and pierce it in 4–5 vertical lines running down the length of the matzo. Repeat with remaining pieces of dough.

Bake for 20–25 minutes on each side on a parchment-lined baking sheet. Ideally you would want to bake a few at a time since each baking session is around 40 minutes or so. Once the matzo is baked until crispy, remove and allow it to cool slightly before serving.

Note: Kosher laws require that seder matzo be made out of 1 of 5 grains in order to be acceptable for Passover. So technically this version is not kosher for Passover but is still a great alternative if you cannot have grains.

Bubbe's tip: New to yuca? It can be a little tricky in the beginning, but if you have a tamper, use it! This will help yield a beautiful dough.

Cassava Matzo

This matzo recipe uses cassava flour instead of cassava root, for a quicker preparation.
It is thin, crispy and makes a delicious matzo brei too!

Prep Time: 10 minutes   Cook Time: 6–8 minutes   Makes: 5 servings

1 cup (122 g) cassava flour (not tapioca)

1 cup (185 g) potato starch

3 tablespoons (45 ml) avocado oil or olive oil

¾ cup + 1 tablespoon (190 ml) water

1 tablespoon (15 ml) honey

Sea salt to taste

Preheat your oven to 475°F (246°C). Combine all ingredients in a medium-sized mixing bowl. Stir the ingredients to combine, and then mix by hand to form a ball of dough.

Divide the dough into four equal pieces. Roll out each piece of dough on a lightly floured piece of parchment paper (using the potato starch to dust) into a rectangle, approximately 8 x 6 inch (20 x 15 cm). You will want to make the rolled out matzo as thin as possible; this will help it be both crispy and bubbled in texture.

Transfer the parchment paper and unbaked matzo onto a baking sheet. Poke holes vertically in the matzo with fork prongs, as shown in the photograph, and then bake for 3 minutes. Remove the baking sheet and turn the matzo over carefully and bake for 3 minutes on the alternate side.

You will want to watch the matzo very carefully so that it does not burn or brown too much; if it does, it will taste burned.

If you need additional cook time per side, bake for no longer than 30 seconds to a minute on each side before flipping and then promptly remove. This means you should bake each piece of matzo for no longer than 8 minutes total. Remove from oven and allow the sheets of matzo to cool slightly before serving.

Note: Kosher laws require that seder matzo be made out of 1 of 5 grains in order to be acceptable for Passover. So technically this version is not kosher for Passover but is still a great alternative if you cannot have grains.

Bubbe's tip: If your matzo is on the thicker side, it will take longer to cook. If it's brown but not yet crisp, turn down the heat to 350°F (176°C) to finish baking.

Pita Bread

Pita bread is the traditional "pocketed" bread, which can be stuffed with tuna salad or used to dip into hummus. This grain-free rendition uses cassava flour instead of wheat flour for an interesting twist on an old favorite!

Prep Time: 10 minutes Cook Time: 10 minutes Makes: 6 servings

1½ cups (350 ml) warm water (around 110°F [43°C])

2 teaspoons (6 g) active dry yeast

1 tablespoon (15 ml) honey or maple syrup

2 cups (245 g) cassava flour

1 teaspoon sea salt

2 tablespoons (30 ml) avocado oil, olive oil or preferred cooking fat

Preheat the oven to 450°F (232°C).

In a mixing bowl, combine the water, yeast and honey and allow it to sit for a few minutes for the yeast to bloom. You'll know the yeast is good when you see it begin to froth or foam. If it doesn't, toss the yeast mixture and begin again.

Once the yeast blooms, add in the flour, salt and oil. Stir with a spoon and then knead by hand until a large ball of dough is formed. Divide the dough into six equal portions. Then take one of them and roll it into a ball. Wet your hands to dampen the dough so that it does not crack when rolled out.

Roll the dough between two pieces of parchment paper, about 5–6 inches (12–15 cm) in diameter. If the dough cracks, use your hands to seal it back together. Remove the top piece of parchment after rolling out.

Cook for 5 minutes on each side, or longer, depending on preference of "pocket" or "dipping" pita.

Bubbe's tip: Prefer more of a pita chip? Roll your dough thinner and bake until crispy! Want a pita pocket? Make it thicker!

Marble Rye Bread

Wait a minute… Isn't rye a grain? And a gluten-containing one at that? It is indeed, which is why there isn't any actual rye in this "rye" bread. Instead, a blend of flours and ground caraway seeds give it the distinctive rye flavor you remember.

Prep Time: 20 minutes, plus 1 hour to rise Cook Time: 20–22 minutes Makes: 1 loaf

2½ teaspoons (17 g) active dry yeast

1 cup (235 ml) warm water (about 110°F [43°C])

2 tablespoons (30 ml) honey, divided

¼ cup (25 g) palm shortening, melted

3 eggs (set one yolk aside for egg wash)

64 grams (⅔ cup) chestnut flour

100 grams (1 cup minus 2 tablespoons) arrowroot

150 grams (1 cup) potato starch

3 tablespoons (45 g) psyllium husk

2 tablespoons (20 g) caraway seeds, ground, plus more for garnish, optional

2 teaspoons (10 g) salt

1 tablespoon (15 ml) molasses

1 teaspoon cocoa powder

1 teaspoon water

Combine the yeast, warm water and 1 tablespoon (15 ml) of the honey in a small bowl. Set aside to bloom—it should get foamy and active and increase in size.

In the bowl of your mixer, beat the melted shortening with eggs, reserving one of the yolks to use later in the egg wash. Beat the shortening and egg mixture for about 30 seconds, or until well mixed.

Whisk together the dry ingredients—chestnut flour through the salt. Add the yeast mixture and dry ingredients to the mixing bowl and beat until well combined, scraping down the sides of the bowl a few times.

Divide the contents into two bowls, about 1¼ cups (340 g) in each. In one bowl, stir in the remaining tablespoon (15 ml) honey. In the other, stir in the molasses, cocoa powder and water.

Cover the bowls with plastic wrap and allow to rise in a warm place for 45 minutes. It will not rise like traditional dough, but will get aerated and increase in size a bit.

Grease a 9 x 5 inch (23 x 13 cm) loaf pan with shortening. After 45 minutes, gently swirl the two doughs together into the prepared pan. Preheat the oven to 375°F (190°C) and allow the dough to rise for another 15 minutes.

Whisk the remaining egg yolk with a drop of water and brush on the dough. Bake for 20–22 minutes, or until the top is browned and forms a good crust. Allow the bread to cool before removing from the pan.

Bubbe's tip: What you want light rye bread instead? Leave out the molasses, cocoa powder and teaspoon of water and add an extra tablespoon (15 ml) of honey to the dough. You don't need to split it in half!

Challah

Nothing smells better than a challah baking. That might be a bold statement, but we're standing by it! This soft warm bread is traditionally served for Shabbat dinner, but after you taste this warm buttery loaf, you will find excuses to make it much more often than once a week!

Prep Time: 15 minutes, plus 1 hour to rise Cook Time: 20–25 minutes Makes: 1 loaf

2½ teaspoons (7 g) yeast

¼ cup (60 ml) warm water (about 110°F [43°C])

3 tablespoons (45 ml) honey, divided

4 eggs

75 g almond flour (scant ¾ cup)

100 g arrowroot powder (heaping ¾ cup)

100 g potato starch (scant ¾ cup)

2 tablespoons (30 g) psyllium husk

¾ teaspoon salt

⅓ cup (80 ml) palm shortening, melted

In a small bowl, combine the yeast, warm water and 1 tablespoon (15 ml) of the honey. Stir to combine and set aside for 5 minutes.

In the bowl of your mixer, beat the eggs until they lighten in color. In a medium bowl, whisk together the almond flour, arrowroot powder, potato starch, psyllium husk and salt. Add the flour mixture, shortening and remaining honey to the eggs and beat until well combined.

Mix in the yeast mixture and beat until well combined, scraping down the sides a couple of times.

The dough will not be like a traditional bread dough, it will be more like cake batter.

Cover the bowl with a clean, dry towel and place in a warm, draft-free place to rise for 45 minutes. After an hour, preheat the oven to 350°F (177°C) and grease a 9 x 5 inch (23 x 13 cm) loaf pan. Give the dough a stir and pour it into the pan. Let it rise again, for 15 minutes or so, until it fills about two-thirds of the pan.

Bake for 20–25 minutes, until cooked through and golden brown. Allow the bread to cool before removing from the pan.

Bubbe's tip: In my day, we braided our challah and ate it every Shabbat. If you must have it braided, you can find a mold on that computer you're always on.

Bialys

Bialys don't get nearly as much love as their popular cousin, the bagel, but are definitely worth knowing. Make sure you plan ahead when you make them—you'll need to let the starter do its thing for 8–24 hours.

Prep Time: 20 minutes, plus 45 minutes to rise and 8–24 hours to ferment   Cook Time: 16–20 minutes
Makes: 6 bialys

FOR THE STARTER

1 teaspoon (3 g) yeast

¼ cup (30 g) cassava flour

½ cup (120 ml) water

FOR THE BIALYS

½ cup (120 ml) water

2 teaspoons (6 g) yeast

1 teaspoon (5 ml) honey

1 egg + 1 white

160 g (1½ cups) almond flour

100 g (¾ cup + 2 tablespoons) cassava flour

75 g (½ cup) potato starch, plus more for forming bialys

1 tablespoon (15 g) psyllium husk

1 teaspoon salt

½ medium onion, cut into small dices

2 teaspoons (10 ml) olive or avocado oil

1 teaspoon (3 g) poppy seeds

Coarse sea salt, optional

Combine the starter ingredients and stir to combine. Cover with plastic wrap and allow the mixture to sit at room temperature for at least 8 hours, and up to 24.

After the starter has sat for 8–24 hours, combine the water, yeast and honey in a small bowl. Set aside for 5 minutes, or until it becomes foamy and active.

With a handheld or stand mixer, beat the eggs until they're frothy and lighter in color, about 2 minutes. To them, add the almond flour, cassava flour, potato starch, psyllium husk and salt, along with the starter and yeast mixture.

Beat the mixture on high for 2–3 minutes. It should form a very sticky dough. Liberally dust a work surface with potato starch and turn the dough onto it. With floured hands, divide the dough into six portions and form each into a disc, about an inch (2.5 cm) thick. Place on a parchment-lined baking sheet and cover with plastic wrap. Set aside for 45 minutes in a warm, draft-free place.

Meanwhile, sauté the onions in the oil over medium-high heat until golden brown, about 6–8 minutes.

After the bialys have risen, make an indentation in the center, about 1 inch (2.5 cm). Liberally brush the tops of the bialys with water. Fill the indentation with the onions, and sprinkle with poppy seeds and coarse salt, if using.

Bake them for 10–12 minutes, or until they spring back to the touch. To brown the tops, place under a broiler for 2 minutes, or until golden brown.

Bubbe's tip: You won't be able to still call it a bialy, but if you want more of a roll, skip the indentation and the onions and you'll have a good sandwich roll. I'll take mine with chopped liver.

Plain Bagels

What happens when two Jews have to be grain-free for health reasons?
Well first, they lock themselves in the kitchen until they crack the code for bagels they can eat!
These are as good as the real thing and far better than any gluten-free bagel you can buy.

Prep Time: 10 minutes Cook Time: 30 minutes Makes: 6 bagels

Water for boiling

1 tablespoon (15 ml) apple cider vinegar

Light olive oil or coconut oil for greasing the parchment-lined baking sheet

2½ teaspoons (7 g) active yeast

2 tablespoons (30 ml) honey

1 cup (240 ml) warm water (about 110°F [43°C])

1 cup (90 g) blanched almond flour

1 cup (130 g) cassava flour, plus more if needed

¾ cup (100 g) potato starch

1 rounded teaspoon sea salt

Bubbe's tip: My little bubula, remember cassava flour is different from tapioca starch. To read more about this, be sure to refer to the resources page (page 246)!

Bring a large pot of water to a boil and add in the apple cider vinegar. Preheat your oven to 450°F (232°C). Liberally grease a parchment-lined baking sheet with the oil.

Combine the yeast, honey and warm water in a large bowl and whisk to combine. Allow to sit for 5 minutes, or until the mixture becomes foamy and active. If that doesn't happen, toss it and start over—it means either the yeast is a dud or too old, or the water was too hot or too cold.

In a medium bowl, whisk together the almond flour, cassava flour, potato starch and salt. Add to the yeast mixture and stir to combine. The consistency of the dough should be more like clay than a traditional dough. The perfect texture for these is just dry enough to work with, but still a little sticky. If that's the case, divide the dough into six portions. If not, add a tablespoon at a time of either water (15 ml) or cassava flour (8 g), depending on whether it's too wet or too dry, until it's the right consistency.

There are two ways to form the bagel shape. Either way, wet your hands before handling the dough and work on a surface liberally dusted with cassava flour.

A. Roll into a snake shape with slightly tapered edges, and bring those edges together.

Or

B. Roll each portion into a ball and stick your thumb through the center, creating a hole and stretching the dough to be bagel-shaped.

Once the water is boiling, turn it down slightly so it's at a strong simmer. Drop the bagels into the water, 2 or 3 at a time. Use a metal spatula to get them off the counter if they don't keep their shape when you try to lift them.

Once the bagels float, boil them for 4 minutes.

Transfer the bagels to the prepared baking sheet. Bake for 20–25 minutes, or until golden brown.

Allow the bagels to rest for 30 minutes before slicing. Yes, this is difficult, but consider it a necessary step, or else the bagels will be gummy when you cut them.

These are best toasted, and also freeze and reheat wonderfully.

Everything Bagels

If "Jewish" was a food, it might possibly be an Everything Bagel. This bagel is our star performer, as its texture is as close to an East Coast bagel as you can get without adding back in grain and gluten. Even grain eaters have celebrated this bagel!

Prep Time: 10 minutes   Cook Time: 30 minutes   Makes: 6 bagels

Water for boiling

1 tablespoon (15 ml) apple cider vinegar

Light olive oil or coconut oil for greasing the parchment-lined baking sheet

2½ teaspoons (7 g) active yeast

2 tablespoons (30 ml) honey

1 cup (240 ml) warm water (about 110°F [43°C])

1 cup (90 g) blanched almond flour

1 cup (130 g) cassava flour

¾ cup (100 g) potato starch

3 tablespoons (38 g) minced onion, divided

1 teaspoon garlic powder

1 rounded teaspoon sea salt

1 tablespoon (9 g) poppy seeds

1 tablespoon (10 g) sesame seeds

1 tablespoon (12 g) coarse sea salt

1 tablespoon (10 g) caraway seeds, optional

Bubbe's tip: My little bubula, remember cassava flour is different from tapioca starch. To read more about this, be sure to refer to the resources page (page 246)!

Bring a large pot of water to a boil and add in the apple cider vinegar. Preheat your oven to 450°F (232°C). Liberally grease a parchment-lined baking sheet with oil.

Combine the yeast, honey and warm water in a large bowl and whisk to combine. Allow to sit for 5 minutes, or until the mixture becomes foamy and active. If that doesn't happen, toss it and start over—it means either the yeast is a dud or too old, or the water was too hot or too cold.

In a medium bowl, whisk together the almond flour, cassava flour, potato starch, 2 tablespoons (25 g) of the minced onion, garlic powder and salt. Add to the yeast mixture and stir to combine. The consistency of the dough should be more like clay than a traditional dough. The perfect texture for these is just dry enough to work with, but still a little sticky. If that's the case, divide the dough into six portions. If not, add a tablespoon at a time of either water (15 ml) or cassava flour (8 g), depending on whether it's too wet or too dry, until it's the right consistency.

There are two ways to form the bagel shape. Either way, wet your hands before handling the dough and work on a surface liberally dusted with cassava flour.

A. Roll into a snake shape with slightly tapered edges, and bring those edges together.

Or

B. Roll each portion into a ball and stick your thumb through the center, creating a hole and stretching the dough to be bagel-shaped.

Once the water is boiling, turn it down slightly so it's at a strong simmer. Drop the bagels into the water, 2 or 3 at a time. Use a metal spatula to get them off the counter if they don't keep their shape when you try to lift them.

Once the bagels float, boil them for 4 minutes.

Transfer the bagels to the prepared baking sheet and sprinkle remaining tablespoon (12 g) of onions, poppy seeds, sesame seeds, coarse salt and caraway seeds on top. Bake for 20–25 minutes, or until golden brown.

Allow the bagels to rest for 30 minutes before slicing. Yes, this is difficult, but consider it a necessary step, or else the bagels will be gummy when you cut them.

These are best toasted, and also freeze and reheat wonderfully.

Chocolate Chip Bagels

For those with a sweet tooth, chocolate chip bagels are the perfect combination between a crispy, chewy, authentic bagel and a tasty treat! Put on a schmear of dairy-free butter or cashew cream cheese, and suddenly you've conquered all your cravings in a single baked good.

Prep Time: 10 minutes   Cook Time: 30–35 minutes   Makes: 6 bagels

Water for boiling

1 tablespoon (15 ml) apple cider vinegar

Light olive oil or coconut oil for greasing the parchment-lined baking sheet

2½ teaspoons (7 g) active yeast

¼ cup (60 ml) maple syrup

1 cup (240 ml) warm water (about 110°F [43°C])

1 cup (90 g) blanched almond flour

1 cup (130 g) cassava flour

¾ cup (100 g) potato starch

1 rounded teaspoon sea salt

½ cup (120 g) chocolate chips (you can add as many or as few as you like)

Bubbe's tip: My little bubula, remember cassava flour is different from tapioca starch. To read more about this, be sure to refer to the resources page (page 246)!

Bring a large pot of water to a boil and add the apple cider vinegar. Preheat your oven to 450°F (232°C). Liberally grease a parchment-lined baking sheet with the olive or coconut oil.

Combine the yeast, maple syrup and warm water in a large bowl and whisk to combine. Allow to sit for 5 minutes, or until the mixture becomes foamy and active. If that doesn't happen, toss it and start over—it means either the yeast is a dud or too old, or the water was too hot or too cold.

In a medium bowl, whisk together the almond flour, cassava flour, potato starch and salt. Add to the yeast mixture and stir to combine. The consistency of the dough should be more like clay than a traditional dough. The perfect texture for these is just dry enough to work with, but still a little sticky. If that's the case, divide the dough into six portions. If not, add a tablespoon at a time of either water (15 ml) or cassava flour (8 g), depending on whether it's too wet or too dry, until it's the right consistency. Then, mix in your chocolate chips and combine well. You'll want these to be thoroughly incorporated.

There are two ways to form the bagel shape. Either way, wet your hands before handling the dough and work on a surface liberally dusted with cassava flour.

A. Roll into a snake shape with slightly tapered edges, and bring those edges together.

Or

B. Roll each portion into a ball and stick your thumb through the center, creating a hole and stretching the dough to be bagel-shaped.

Once the water is boiling, turn it down slightly so it's at a strong simmer. Drop the bagels into the water, 2 or 3 at a time. Use a metal spatula to get them off the counter if they don't keep their shape when you try to lift them.

Once the bagels float, boil them for 4 minutes.

Transfer the bagels to the prepared baking sheet. Bake for 20–25 minutes, or until golden brown.

Allow the bagels to rest for 30 minutes before slicing. Yes, this is difficult, but consider it a necessary step, or else the bagels will be gummy when you cut them.

These are best toasted, and also freeze and reheat wonderfully.

Cinnamon Raisin Bagels

This recipe is the junction where a delicious cinnamon kugel meets a perfectly boiled-then-baked bagel. Slightly sweetened with maple syrup instead of refined sugar, your body will be thanking you bite after bite.

Prep Time: 10 minutes **Cook Time:** 30–35 minutes **Makes:** 6 bagels

Water for boiling

1 tablespoon (15 ml) apple cider vinegar

Light olive oil or coconut oil for greasing the parchment-lined baking sheet

2½ teaspoons (7 g) active yeast

¼ cup (60 ml) maple syrup

1 cup (240 ml) warm water (about 110°F [43°C])

1 cup (90 g) blanched almond flour

1 cup (130 g) cassava flour

¾ cup (100 g) potato starch

1 rounded teaspoon sea salt

½ cup (120 g) organic raisins (you can add as many or as few as you like)

1 teaspoon ground cinnamon

Bubbe's tip: My little bubula, remember cassava flour is different from tapioca starch. To read more about this, be sure to refer to the resources page (page 246)!

Bring a large pot of water to a boil and add the apple cider vinegar. Preheat your oven to 450°F (232°C). Liberally grease a parchment-lined baking sheet with the oil.

Combine the yeast, maple syrup and warm water in a large bowl and whisk to combine. Allow to sit for 5 minutes, or until the mixture becomes foamy and active. If that doesn't happen, toss it and start over—it means either the yeast is a dud or too old, or the water was too hot or too cold.

In a medium bowl, whisk together the almond flour, cassava flour, potato starch and salt. Add to the yeast mixture and stir to combine. The consistency of the dough should be more like clay than a traditional dough. The perfect texture for these is just dry enough to work with, but still a little sticky. If that's the case, divide the dough into six portions. If not, add a tablespoon at a time of either water (15 ml) or cassava flour (8 g), depending on whether it's too wet or too dry, until it's the right consistency. Then, mix in your raisins and cinnamon and combine well. You'll want these to be thoroughly incorporated.

There are two ways to form the bagel shape. Either way, wet your hands before handling the dough and work on a surface liberally dusted with cassava flour.

A. Roll into a snake shape with slightly tapered edges, and bring those edges together.

Or

B. Roll each portion into a ball and stick your thumb through the center, creating a hole and stretching the dough to be bagel-shaped.

Once the water is boiling, turn it down slightly so it's at a strong simmer. Drop the bagels into the water, 2 or 3 at a time. Use a metal spatula to get them off the counter if they don't keep their shape when you try to lift them.

Once the bagels float, boil them for 4 minutes.

Transfer the bagels to the prepared baking sheet. Bake for 20–25 minutes, or until golden brown.

Allow the bagels to rest for 30 minutes before slicing. Yes, this is difficult, but consider it a necessary step, or else the bagels will be gummy when you cut them.

These are best toasted and also freeze and reheat wonderfully.

Allergen Friendly Bagels
(Nightshade-, Egg-, Nut- and Grain-Free)

This bagel recipe takes our "almost famous" grain-free bagel recipe and adapts it for those who have more extreme food sensitivities. In this one you will not find nightshades, eggs, nuts, grains or dairy! Make sure you follow Bubbe's tip for this one so you can get the best possible result!

Prep Time: 10 minutes Cook Time: 30–35 minutes Makes: 6 bagels

Water for boiling

1 tablespoon (15 ml) apple cider vinegar

Light olive oil or coconut oil for greasing the parchment-lined baking sheet

2½ teaspoons (7 g) active yeast

1 tablespoon (15 ml) honey

1 cup (240 ml) warm water (about 110°F [43°C])

1 cup (130 g) cassava flour

½ cup (115 g) coconut flour

½ teaspoon sea salt

Dried minced onion, garlic powder, poppy seeds and caraway seeds, if tolerated, optional

Bubbe's tip: These are slightly different in texture than my original bagel recipe, but don't schvitz! If you want the best result, start slicing with a serrated knife after the bagel cools and then pull the halves apart before slicing all the way through. This will create more "crumb" before toasting!

Bring a large pot of water to a boil and add in the apple cider vinegar. Preheat your oven to 450°F (232°C). Liberally grease a parchment-lined baking sheet with the oil.

Combine the yeast, honey and warm water in a large bowl and whisk to combine. Allow to sit for 5 minutes, or until the mixture becomes foamy and active. If that doesn't happen, toss it and start over—it means either the yeast is a dud or too old, or the water was too hot or too cold.

In a medium bowl, whisk together the cassava flour, coconut flour and salt. Add to the yeast mixture and stir to combine. The consistency of the dough should be more like clay than a traditional dough. The perfect texture for these is just dry enough to work with, but still a little sticky. If that's the case, divide the dough into six portions. If not, add a tablespoon at a time of either water (15 ml) or cassava flour (8 g), depending on whether it's too wet or too dry, until it's the right consistency.

There are two ways to form the bagel shape. Either way, wet your hands before handling the dough and work on a surface liberally dusted with cassava flour.

A. Roll into a snake shape with slightly tapered edges, and bring those edges together.

Or

B. Roll each portion into a ball and stick your thumb through the center, creating a hole and stretching the dough to be bagel-shaped.

Once the water is boiling, turn it down slightly so it's at a strong simmer. Drop the bagels into the water, 2 or 3 at a time. Use a metal spatula to get them off the counter if they don't keep their shape when you try to lift them.

Once the bagels float, boil them for 4 minutes.

Remove the bagels with a slotted spoon or skimmer and place them on your parchment-lined baking sheet.

If you are adding seeds and minced onion, you can sprinkle those on top at this time.

Bake the bagels for 20–25 minutes.

Allow the bagels to rest for 30 minutes before slicing. Yes, this is difficult, but consider it a necessary step, or else the bagels will be gummy when you cut them.

These are best toasted and also freeze and reheat wonderfully.

Not-So-Traditional Deli Fare

I remember the first time I pulled up to a Reuben the size of the Old Testament. I could never eat all that corned beef, but I sure tried. The memory of that sammy is what gave me the chutzpah to want to make foods that people love. If you don't want to schlep all that leftover deli goodness home, why not make it yourself? In this chapter we've given you three types of Matzo Brei, traditional Egg Salad, Tuna Salad and Whitefish Salad, along with three kinds of Knishes and two kinds of homemade pickles. And what, you think you're too old to enjoy a Bagel Dog?! Feh! Never! You won't believe how much more delicious your deli fare can be when you make it at home with heart.

Challah French Toast

Happen to have an extra loaf of challah? You should if only so you can make Challah French Toast for brunch. You certainly don't have to be Jewish to know this recipe is a knock out!

Prep Time: 10 minutes (if your challah is already baked) **Cook Time:** 16–20 minutes **Makes:** 4 servings

6 eggs

¼ cup (60 ml) orange juice

½ cup (120 ml) full-fat canned coconut milk

1 tablespoon (15 ml) vanilla

1 teaspoon ground cinnamon

⅛ teaspoon sea salt

1 loaf Challah (page 52)

2 tablespoons (30 ml) ghee or oil, for frying

In a large, shallow baking dish, beat together the eggs, orange juice, coconut milk, vanilla, cinnamon and sea salt.

Slice the challah into 10–12 slices and place into the dish with the egg batter. Allow them to sit for 10–15 minutes, flipping several times.

Heat a large skillet over medium heat and melt 1 tablespoon (15 ml) of the ghee. Once sizzling, fry the French toast in batches for about 2 minutes per side, or until golden brown. Repeat with the remaining slices, adding more ghee to the pan as needed.

Bubbe's tip: If your challah is a day or two old and on the dry side, just let it soak longer in the egg mixture. Maybe clean the house while you wait. You never know when family will stop by for a visit.

Lox and Onion Eggs

Getting bored with regular old scrambled eggs? This should fix that.

Prep Time: 5 minutes Cook Time: 10–13 minutes Makes: 4 servings

1 tablespoon (15 ml) olive oil

1 medium onion, cut into small dices

8 large eggs

½ teaspoon salt

Pinch black pepper

¼ pound (113 g) Lox (page 81)

Heat a large skillet over medium high heat and add the oil. Once hot, add the onions and sauté for 8–10 minutes, or until golden brown and beginning to soften.

Meanwhile, whisk the eggs with the salt and pepper. Once the onions are golden brown, add the eggs to the pan. Once they start to set on the bottom, add the lox and scramble into the eggs. Cook until just set, about 2–3 minutes, or until cooked to your liking.

Bubbe's tip: You want these to be more fancy? You can add whatever you like! Spinach, tomatoes or fresh herbs. The sky is the limit, bubula!

Bagel Dogs

Remember the days of gluten when you could pop into your favorite bagel shop and grab a bagel-wrapped dog? These are just like those, but will make your body so much happier than the originals.

Prep Time: 5 minutes Cook Time: 30 minutes Makes: 4–8 bagel dogs

Water for boiling

1 tablespoon (15 ml) apple cider vinegar

Light olive oil or coconut oil for greasing the parchment-lined baking sheet

2½ teaspoons (7 g) active yeast

2 tablespoons (30 ml) honey

1 cup (240 ml) warm water (about 110°F [43°C])

1 cup (90 g) almond flour

1 cup (130 g) cassava flour

¾ cup (100 g) potato starch

3 tablespoons (38 g) minced onion, divided

1 teaspoon garlic powder

1 rounded teaspoon sea salt

4 large or 8 small 100% beef hot dogs

1 tablespoon (9 g) poppy seeds, or more

1 tablespoon (10 g) sesame seeds, or more

1 tablespoon (12 g) coarse sea salt, or more

1 tablespoon (10 g) caraway seeds, optional

Bring a large pot of water to a boil and add in the apple cider vinegar. Preheat your oven to 450°F (232°C). Liberally grease a parchment-lined baking sheet with oil.

Combine the yeast, honey and warm water in a large bowl and whisk to combine. Allow to sit for 5 minutes, or until the mixture becomes foamy and active. If that doesn't happen, toss it and start over—it means either the yeast is a dud or too old, or the water was too hot or too cold.

In a medium bowl, whisk together the almond flour, cassava flour, potato starch, 2 tablespoons (25 g) of the minced onion, garlic powder and salt. Add to the yeast mixture and stir to combine. The consistency of the dough should be more like clay than a traditional dough. The perfect texture for these is just dry enough to work with, but still a little sticky. If that's the case, divide the dough into equal portions, depending on the number of dogs you're making. If not, add a tablespoon at a time of either water (15 ml) or cassava flour (8 g), depending on whether it's too wet or too dry, until it's the right consistency.

Take one of the portions of dough and either roll it out like a long snake or into a ball, depending on how you'd like your bagel dogs to look.

Take one grass-fed hot dog and dry it off in case it is wet and wrap the dough around it in a spiral shape. If the dough breaks, seal it back together with a dampened hand—it does not have to be perfectly formed.

If you use one large ball of dough instead of a spiral (rolled out snake), just wrap the dough around the hot dog until it makes one large "bun" and seal it shut by pressing it together on the underneath side. Wrap all of the remaining dogs.

Drop the dough-wrapped dogs 1 or 2 at a time into the boiling water for about 5 minutes. Remove with a slotted spoon and transfer to your baking sheet.

Sprinkle with remaining minced onion and the poppy seeds, sesame seeds, salt and caraway seeds (if using). Bake for about 15 minutes; be careful not to overbake. To reheat, toast on low in a toaster oven.

Bubbe's tip: Keeping kosher? Not all dogs are created equally! Ideally, you want kosher and grass-fed, so read the labels!

Sweet Matzo Brei

This Sweet Matzo Brei is made of scrambled eggs, grain-free matzo and a drizzle of real maple syrup to create a healthy version of an old favorite. Your leftover Passover matzo has a new home, and it's in this "French-toasty" delicious dish!

Prep Time: 5 minutes   Cook Time: 5 minutes   Makes: 1 serving

2 eggs

2 tablespoons (30 ml) full-fat coconut milk

1 teaspoon maple syrup

Pinch sea salt

1 sheet Matzo (see page 44 or 47), broken into bite-sized pieces

1 tablespoon (15 ml) Dairy-Free Butter (see page 227), avocado oil or coconut oil

FOR SERVING
Sliced strawberry
Coconut palm sugar to taste

In a medium bowl, beat the eggs with the coconut milk, maple syrup and salt. Mix in the broken matzo.

In a medium-sized skillet, heat the butter (or cooking fat) over medium-high heat for about a minute.

Pour in the egg and matzo mixture, shifting the eggs with a spatula as they cook, to prevent burning. Cook for a total of 3–4 minutes, or until the eggs are cooked through and the matzo is slightly toasted.

Remove from the skillet and garnish with a fresh strawberry or a sprinkle of coconut palm sugar.

Bubbe's tip: There are several methods to making a great matzo brei; with this one, be sure not to soak the grain-free matzo too long or it will become a soggy dreck. Trust me, would you!?

Savory Matzo Brei

Ask whether matzo brei should be savory or sweet and it's like asking if matzo balls should be "floaters" or "sinkers." This question is age old and can certainly spark a debate. This savory version combines red pepper, onion and spinach and is topped off with fresh chives.

Prep Time: 10 minutes Cook Time: 20 minutes Makes: 4 servings

8 pastured eggs

¼ cup (60 ml) baby spinach leaves, chopped

½ teaspoon sea salt, plus coarse sea salt for garnishing

¼ teaspoon celery salt

½ teaspoon ground black pepper

¾ teaspoon onion powder

2 tablespoons (30 ml) olive or avocado oil or Schmaltz (page 235)

1 red bell pepper, diced

1 onion, diced

4 sheets Matzo (page 44 or 47), broken into bite-sized pieces

¼ cup (60 ml) flax, coconut, almond or other dairy-free milk

Fresh chives to garnish

Crack the eggs into a medium-sized mixing bowl and whisk them until they are well combined. Next, add in the spinach, sea salt, celery salt, black pepper and onion powder and whisk once more. Set the bowl aside. Then, begin heating the cooking fat over medium/high heat in a large skillet. Add in the red pepper and onion and cook until the vegetables are softened and the onion is translucent, about 5 minutes. Add the matzo to the egg mixture, along with dairy-free milk. Stir to combine and then pour the egg mixture into the skillet.

Lower the heat to medium, so as not to burn the eggs, and shift the mixture around until the eggs are cooked through, about 3–4 minutes. They will basically be scrambled in texture with the bits of matzo cooked inside the mixture. Garnish with fresh chives.

Bubbe's tip: If you want your matzo to stay slightly crisped, do not soak it too long or you will have a soggy disappointment!

Fluffy Matzo Brei

Separating the eggs in this recipe will result in a light and fluffy matzo brei.
Depending on what kind of matzo you use, soaking might not be necessary, or might take less time.
If using store bought, skip the soaking step, and just mix the matzo with the egg yolks.

Prep Time: 5–15 minutes Cook Time: 6–8 minutes Makes: 1 serving

1 sheet Matzo (page 44 or 47)
2 eggs, separated
½ teaspoon vanilla extract
1 teaspoon maple syrup
Dash cinnamon
Pinch salt
2 teaspoons (10 ml) coconut or avocado oil
Maple syrup, for serving

Break up the matzo into bite-sized pieces and place in a bowl. Cover with water and set aside for 10–15 minutes, or until soft. You can test it by removing a piece and breaking it in half. If it snaps like it did before soaking, give it a little bit longer.

Meanwhile, beat the egg whites until stiff peaks form. In a separate bowl, beat the yolks with the vanilla, maple syrup, cinnamon and salt.

Once the matzo has soaked, use your hands to squeeze out the water and place the matzo into the egg yolk mixture. Stir to combine, and then gently fold in the whites.

Heat a small skillet over medium heat and add the oil. (A non-stick or well-seasoned, cast-iron skillet works best for this.) Once it shimmers, pour in the matzo brei mixture. Cook for 3–4 minutes before flipping and cooking an additional 3–4 minutes on the other side. Serve with maple syrup.

Bubbe's tip: Don't like maple syrup? This matzo brei is also delicious with fresh or cooked fruit!

Lox

Good lox is a thing of beauty. When you discover just how easy it is to make at home,
you might never buy the subpar, packaged stuff again!

Prep Time: 5 minutes Cook Time: 48 hours to cure Makes: 6–8 servings

½ cup (100 g) sugar
4 tablespoons (72 g) kosher salt
2 tablespoons (30 g) smoked salt
1 pound (450 g) very fresh salmon

In a small bowl, combine sugar, kosher salt and smoked salt. Divide the mixture in half and with one half, coat the salmon on all sides, packing it on as well as you can. Wrap tightly with plastic wrap, leaving one end open. Set aside the remaining salt mixture.

Place in a baking dish and put some weight on top of it: for example, a plate or a small cast iron pan with a can on top. Place a folded towel under the baking dish so it's at an angle; this will allow the excess liquid to drain from the salmon. Make sure the open end of the plastic wrap is at the lower end of the dish.

Leave refrigerated for 24 hours and then unwrap the salmon. Pack the rest of the salt mixture onto it. Using new plastic wrap, re-wrap and place back in the fridge, in the same manner you did the first time for another 24 hours.

After the second 24 hours, unwrap the salmon and rinse with cold water. Pat it dry. With a long, thin knife, slice against the grain at an angle as thinly as possible, ideally shortly before eating.

Keep the lox tightly wrapped in the fridge, and enjoy within five days.

Bubbe's tip: Worried about the sugar used in this recipe? Only a bisl remains in the salmon and the rest gets rinsed off.

Pastrami

When curing brisket for pastrami, pink curing salt is commonly used. Although harmless when used correctly, it contains red dye, which is a bit of a deal breaker. While it's not necessary to the curing process, it does help keep the meat pink instead of brown when cooked. Using beet juice helps give the pastrami that pink color we're used to seeing, but the end result will be wonderful, whether or not you use it. Pastrami is similar to corned beef in flavor and is absolutely delicious as part of a Reuben sammy (page 101).

Prep Time: 10 minutes plus 4–5 days to brine Cook Time: 4–5 hours Makes: 6–8 servings

3 quarts (2.8 L) water, divided

1 cup (288 g) kosher salt

5 garlic cloves, smashed and chopped

½ cup (120 ml) honey

2 tablespoons (20 g) pickling spice

2 cups (435 g) ice

½ cup (120 ml) beet juice, optional

4–5 pounds (1.8–2.2 kg) beef brisket

2 tablespoons (14 g) black peppercorns, toasted and ground

2 tablespoons (11 g) coriander, toasted and ground

1 tablespoon (7 g) smoked paprika

In a medium saucepan, boil 1 quart (950 ml) of the water and add the salt, garlic, honey and pickling spice. Stir to dissolve the salt. Combine with the remaining 2 quarts (1.9 L) of water, ice and beet juice, if using. Pour it into a container that has a tight-fitting lid and will fit the brine and pastrami. Allow it to cool completely before adding the brisket.

Trim the brisket of any excess fat, but make sure to leave about ¼ inch (6 mm) on the top. Once the brining solution is cooled completely, add the brisket, cover the container and refrigerate.

Allow the brisket to brine for 4–5 days, turning it daily if it is not evenly submerged in the brine. After 4–5 days, remove the brisket, rinse and pat dry. Allow it to come to room temperature for about an hour.

Preheat the oven to 250°F (121°C) and prepare a large roasting pan with a rack.

Combine the ground pepper, coriander and smoked paprika in a small bowl. Once the meat is room temperature, place it fat side down on the rack. Pat about half of the spice mixture onto the meat, trying to get as much to stick as possible. Flip the brisket and repeat on the other side. Pour 2 cups (475 ml) of water into the roasting pan and cover tightly with two layers of aluminum foil.

Cook for 4–5 hours, about 1 hour to 75 minutes per pound of brisket. Allow the brisket to rest for at least 20 minutes before slicing.

To reheat the pastrami: Place thin slices in a small pan with a bit of water and cover. Heat on medium-high for 2–3 minutes, or until heated through.

Bubbe's tip: What, you like corned beef for your Reubens instead of pastrami? That's easy. After brining the brisket, simmer it in water with some carrots and onion for 2½–3 hours instead of cooking it in the oven.

Cranberry Crunch Tuna Salad

This easy tuna salad is perfect for a simple lunch or for breaking the fast after Yom Kippur.
Either way, you'll find it adds a fresh new take to an old classic.

Prep Time: 5 minutes Cook Time: None Makes: 2 servings

2 (5-ounce [284-g]) cans sustainably caught tuna

3–4 tablespoons (48–64 g) Mayonnaise (page 228)

¼ cup (50 g) red onion, minced

¼ cup (30 g) dried, fruit-sweetened cranberries

¼ cup (30 g) toasted pine nuts

¼ cup (30 g) toasted sunflower seeds or chopped pecan pieces, optional

Simply mix all ingredients in a bowl and use a fork to combine well. Serve on an Everything Bagel (page 59) or on Matzo (page 44 or 47).

Bubbe's tip: What, you need easier than this? Then have your cat make it while you sip on some Manischewitz.

Curried Egg Salad

This egg salad offers a little more oomph with its added curry sprinkle. Combined with the Dijon, mayo and eggs, it provides a great alternative to the standard edition.

Prep Time: 5 minutes Cook Time: 12 minutes Makes: 4 servings

7 eggs
1 teaspoon Dijon mustard
⅛ teaspoon celery salt
¼ teaspoon onion powder
¼ teaspoon garlic powder
¾ teaspoon curry powder
¼ teaspoon sea salt
1 tablespoon (12 g) dried minced onion
⅓ cup (75 g) Mayonnaise (page 228)

In a pot that fits a steamer basket, bring a small amount of water to a boil. Put the eggs in the steamer basket and place in the pot. Cover, and allow to steam for 12 minutes.

After 12 minutes, carefully remove the basket and dunk the eggs into cold water to cool. Gently crack the eggs all over and peel.

Chop the eggs and place them in a mixing bowl. Add all the remaining ingredients and stir to combine. Chill until ready to serve.

Bubbe's tip: Bubula, did you know you could bake eggs too?! It's true! Just fill a standard muffin tin with eggs and bake for 30 minutes at 350°F (177°). Could it get any easier?!

Smoked Whitefish Salad

If you're getting bored with tuna salad, Smoked Whitefish Salad is a great way to mix it up!

Prep Time: 5 minutes   Cooking Time: None   Makes: 2 servings as a meal, 6–8 as an appetizer

2 cups (230 g) smoked whitefish, bones removed

3 tablespoons (10 g) very finely diced red onion

1 tablespoon (15 ml) lemon juice

1 teaspoon fresh minced dill, or ¼ teaspoon dried, plus more for garnish, optional

½ cup (128 g) Mayonnaise (page 228)

Salt to taste (depends on the saltiness of your whitefish, you may not need any)

Combine all ingredients in a medium mixing bowl and stir well to combine. Garnish with additional dill, if desired.

Bubbe's tip: Any hot-smoked fish will work in this recipe—mackerel, trout or even salmon!

Caramelized Onion and Potato Knish

Knish is the essence of street food; portable, filling and unbelievably tasty. The two classic varieties are simple potato and potato with spinach. Whichever one your prefer, don't forget the mustard!

Prep Time: 20 minutes Cook Time: About 90 minutes Makes: 8 servings

1 cup (130 g) cassava flour
¼ teaspoon baking soda
1 teaspoon psyllium husk
¼ teaspoon salt
1 egg, separated
¼ cup (60 ml) Schmaltz (page 235) or shortening, melted
½ teaspoon apple cider vinegar
½ cup (120 ml) lukewarm water

FOR POTATO FILLING

2 tablespoons (30 ml) Schmaltz (page 235) or olive oil, divided
1 small onion, sliced
1 large russet potato
½ teaspoon salt
1 cup (180 g) packed cooked spinach, drained and water squeezed out, optional
Mustard, for serving

Mix together the flour, baking soda, psyllium husk and salt. In a separate bowl, whisk together the egg white, schmaltz, apple cider vinegar and water.

Combine the wet and dry ingredients and knead into a dough. It should be kneadable, but slightly tacky. Place in a small bowl and cover with plastic wrap. Set aside and let rest for 45 minutes to 1 hour.

Meanwhile, in a medium saucepan, heat 1 tablespoon (15 ml) of the schmaltz or olive oil over medium heat and add the sliced onions. Turn the heat down to medium-low and sauté until deeply brown and very soft, about 45 minutes.

Peel and slice the potatoes into 1-inch (2.5-cm) slices and place in a medium pot and cover with water and a pinch of salt. Bring to a boil and cook until soft, about 20 minutes. Drain the potatoes and allow them to cool slightly. Once the onions are caramelized, mash them in with the potatoes, along with the remaining schmaltz or olive oil and the salt. For a spinach knish add the spinach now.

Preheat the oven to 375°F (190°C) and line a baking sheet with parchment paper.

Divide the dough into two halves and roll one half out on a sheet of parchment paper until it's a rectangle about 12 x 9 inch (30 x 23 cm). Cut the dough into four sections. Place about ¼ cup (60 ml) of the filling in the center of each rectangle, leaving a half-inch (13-mm) border around the outside. Roll out the remaining dough and cut into four rectangles. Use these to make the tops of the knishes, pressing the ends together and trimming off the extra dough on the outside.

Whisk the egg yolk with a teaspoon (5 ml) of water and brush the knishes with the egg wash.

Transfer the knishes to the prepared baking sheet and brush with the additional beaten egg. Bake for 12 minutes and then flip and bake for an additional 6–8 minutes. Serve with mustard.

Bubbe's tip: I know you like to hurry, bubula, but the onions don't! Don't rush them, or they won't be as delicious for your knishes.

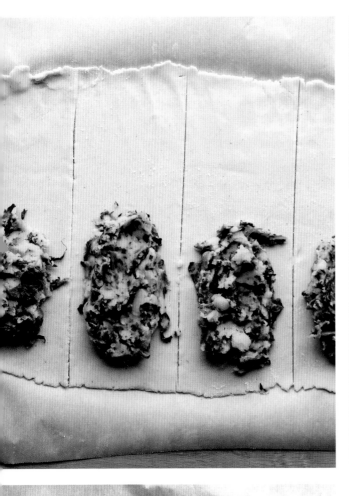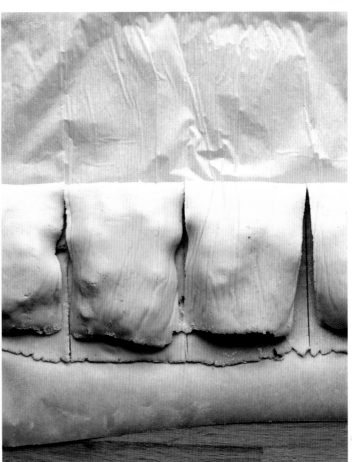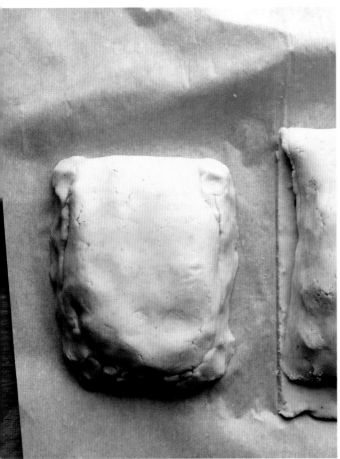

Eggs Florentine with Lox on Everything Bagels

You won't find this dish nestled on top of an English muffin, but you might have found a new favorite anyway! We've brought together lox, spinach, poached eggs, hollandaise and our Everything Bagel (page 59) into one giant party—a bagel Bar Mitzvah if you will.

Prep Time: 10 minutes Cook Time: 10 minutes Makes: 2 servings

2 Everything Bagels (page 59)
3 cups (90 g) baby spinach
4 ounces (113 g) Lox, divided (page 81)
4 eggs

FOR THE HOLLANDAISE
4 pastured egg yolks
2 teaspoons (10 ml) lemon juice
2 tablespoons (30 ml) organic full-fat coconut milk
4 tablespoons (60 ml) light olive oil
⅛ teaspoon sea salt

Pinch paprika for garnishing
Fresh minced chives for garnishing

Slice and toast two everything bagels and lie each one face up on your serving plates.

Next in a small skillet, wilt the spinach leaves by turning the heat on medium-high and allowing the leaves to start sweating out moisture. Once they become softened remove them, leaving the liquid behind, and divide among the 4 bagel halves.

Divide the lox among the 4 bagel halves, arranging on top of the spinach.

The next layer is poached eggs. You may use "poaching cups" if this is a difficult step, or you may cook them using the traditional method. To do this, heat 2 cups (475 ml) of water until simmering (not boiling). Crack your eggs into a small bowl or ramekin and then gently transfer into the water after creating a circular motion in the water with a spoon. You'll want to place the egg in the center of the whirlpool, turn off the heat and cook for around 5 minutes, without touching the egg.

Place the eggs on top of the lox and keep warm.

To make the hollandaise, whisk together the egg yolks and lemon juice vigorously for 2 minutes. Heat the coconut milk and olive oil in a small saucepan over high heat for about a minute, or until heated through. Slowly drizzle the hot oil mix into the egg yolks, whisking vigorously. Once the oil is completely incorporated, add the salt.

Drizzle the warm hollandaise sauce over the poached eggs and garnish with paprika and freshly minced chives.

Bubbe's tip: If poaching eggs makes you a little meshuga, any style will do for this dish, even if you have to scramble them. Don't schvitz the small stuff!!

Fried Potato Knishes

Fried or baked?! Which knish is your favorite? This crispy fried one is dredged in flour instead of wrapped in dough and then goes for a delicious swim in avocado oil.

Prep Time: 10 minutes Cook Time: 30 minutes Makes: 6 servings

1 large onion, diced

1 tablespoon (15 ml) avocado oil or Schmaltz (page 235), plus more for frying

2½ pounds or 4 cups (1.13 kg) peeled, cooked and mashed Yukon gold potatoes

2 eggs

1 teaspoon ground black pepper

1 teaspoon onion powder

1 teaspoon garlic powder

2 teaspoons sea salt, divided

½ cup (58 g) almond flour

½ cup (93 g) potato starch

Mustard, to serve

In a small skillet over medium-high heat, sauté the onion in 1 tablespoon (15 ml) of avocado oil or schmaltz until it is nicely browned, about 8 minutes. While the onion is browning, combine the remaining ingredients (except the mustard) and mix well. You can use your hands for this part to really incorporate the flours with the potato and seasonings. Once the onion is nicely browned, remove it from heat and stir it into the potato mixture.

Heat the additional oil for frying over medium-high heat in a large skillet. Once the oil is glistening (hot enough for frying), make potato patties by hand by first rolling a ball of potato dough and then flattening it into a disc. They can be any size, but keep in mind you'll want them to heat through and be small enough to flip with a flexible spatula without breaking.

Fry the knishes a few at a time, flipping them after 3–4 minutes, or when the underneath side is nicely browned. Once both sides are browned, remove the knishes carefully and arrange them on a towel-lined plate. Serve with mustard of your favorite variety.

Bubbe's tip: You should not stress over these. If you want to make them ahead, it's okay! Just pop them back into the toaster or conventional oven to reheat, and they will crisp again. Now quit schvitzin' like a chazer over it!

Deli Diff Pickles

It's hard to beat a good, old-fashioned, deli-style pickle. Pickling can be an "uncanny" way to revisit memories and also stretch your dollar by preserving a summer harvest. These use a short ferment time and then chill in the fridge for an easy, at-home recipe!

Prep Time: 10 minutes Cook Time: 24 hours to ferment Makes: 5 servings (or more)

2 cups (475 ml) water
½ cup (120 ml) apple cider vinegar
1 teaspoon maple syrup
1 tablespoon (15 g) sea salt
2 tablespoons (19 g) minced garlic
3 dill sprigs
¼ teaspoon red pepper flakes
½ teaspoon dill seed
½ teaspoon whole peppercorns
¼ cup (50 g) dried minced onion
5 Persian cucumbers (sliced if necessary to fit the jar)

Sterilize a quart canning jar either in the dishwasher, or by pouring boiling water in it and pouring it out.

Combine all ingredients except cucumbers in a mixing bowl and set aside. Then, place your cucumbers in a large glass vessel, like a Mason jar, vertically so they all fit snugly, but comfortably.

Pour your liquid mixture into the jar until it covers the cucumbers entirely but leaves about ¼ inch (6 mm) of air at the top.

Cover tightly and allow the jar to sit at room temperature for 24 hours. Then, refrigerate until ready to eat. They get better after a couple of days, so if you are patient wait it out!

Kosher Pickles

You can't have a good deli sandwich without a pickle! These are fermented, which adds some extra probiotic zing to them.

Prep Time: 15 minutes Cook Time: 48 hours to ferment Makes: 6 pickles

2 cups (475 ml) water, divided
1 tablespoon (15 g) salt
1 bay leaf
2 teaspoons (10 ml) pickling spice
2 cloves garlic, peeled and chopped
6 Kirby or Persian cucumbers
1 sprig dill

Sterilize a quart canning jar either in the dishwasher, or by pouring boiling water in it and pouring it out.

In a small saucepan, boil 1 cup (240 ml) of the water and dissolve the salt. Stir in the bay leaf, pickling spice and garlic. Stir in the remaining cup (240 ml) of water.

Pack the cucumbers and dill into the prepared jar and pour the brine over them. Cover with cheesecloth or fabric and secure with a rubber band. Put in a dark place for two days before checking the progress. At this point, you can check one and see if it's fermented to your liking. If so, replace the cloth with a tight fitting lid and refrigerate. If not, leave to ferment for another day or two, checking after each day.

Pastrami Hash

If you've never had Pastrami Hash in a Jewish deli before, you are really missing out.
But don't let that get you too verklempt. It's extremely simple to re-create in your own home. Hash for all!

Prep Time: 10 minutes   Cook Time: 18–20 minutes   Makes: 4 servings

4 Yukon gold potatoes, small-diced

1 onion, diced

1 red pepper, diced

2 tablespoons (30 ml) avocado oil or olive oil

6 ounces (168 g) Pastrami (page 82), diced

½ teaspoon garlic sea salt or more to taste

¼ teaspoon ground black pepper

¼ teaspoon smoked paprika

Optional: 8 eggs, scrambled or sunny-side-up

Start by sautéing the potatoes, onion and red pepper in the cooking fat over medium-high heat for 5 minutes. Then reduce heat to medium, shifting vegetables around so they do not stick to the pan, and cook for another 8–10 minutes, or until the potatoes are soft.

Now add in the pastrami and seasonings and cook for another 5 minutes, or until the pastrami is heated through and the vegetables are at the desired texture. Serve with scrambled or sunny-side-up eggs!

Bubbe's tip: Potatoes take a bit longer to cook than onions do, bubula, so dice them a bit smaller for even cooking! Trust a bubbe, would you?

The Reuben

When you sink your teeth into this grain-free rye bread sandwiching pastrami, homemade Russian dressing and sauerkraut, you'll be transported to a place in time when gluten and dairy were part of your schtick.

Prep Time: None Cook Time: 3–4 minutes Makes: 1 serving

4 ounces (113 g) sliced Pastrami (page 82)

1 tablespoon (15 ml) avocado oil, for toasting the bread

2 slices Marble Rye Bread (page 51)

2 tablespoons (30 ml) Russian Dressing (page 232)

¼ cup (35 g) sauerkraut

Steam the pastrami slices in a small skillet with a bit of water over medium heat until warm, about a minute. Remove from the pan and set aside. Wipe out the pan and add the oil.

Once hot, add the bread and toast for 2–3 minutes, or until crispy and golden. Transfer to a plate and spread on half the Russian dressing. Top with pastrami, sauerkraut, the rest of the dressing and then the remaining slice of bread. Cut in half and serve.

Bubbe's tip: I want that you should love your sandwich! Build it exactly how you want with extra dressing, less meat, more kraut and so on. That shayna punim should be all smiles.

The Rachael

You'll see two different sandwiches called the Rachael, depending on where you are. Sometimes the Reuben is corned beef, and the Rachael is pastrami. But there's a third variation in which the corned beef and kraut are replaced with turkey and crisp slaw.

Prep Time: None   Cook Time: 3–4 minutes   Makes: 1 serving

4 ounces (113 g) sliced turkey

1 tablespoon (15 ml) avocado oil, for toasting the bread

2 slices Marble Rye Bread (page 51)

2 tablespoons (30 ml) Russian Dressing (page 232)

¼ cup (60 g) Dilly Slaw (page 163)

Heat the turkey slices in a small skillet over medium heat until warm, about a minute. Remove from the pan and set aside. Wipe out the pan and add the oil.

Once hot, add the bread and toast for 2–3 minutes, or until crispy and golden. Transfer to a plate and spread on a third of the Russian dressing. Top with turkey, slaw, the rest of the dressing and then the remaining slice of bread. Cut in half and serve.

Bubbe's tip: Going on a picnic? This sandwich is just as good cold! Don't forget to bring the pickles (page 97).

The Jennifer

Jennifer's ideal bagel—so classic, so sophisticated. Just like Jennifer.

Prep Time: 5 minutes Cook Time: None Makes: 1 serving

2 tablespoons (30 g) Cashew Cream Cheese (page 231)

1 Bagel, Plain or Everything (page 56 or 59), sliced and lightly toasted

1 tablespoon (9 g) capers, drained

2 ounces (55 g) or about 3 slices Lox (page 81)

1 thin slice red onion

A few sprigs fresh dill

Spread a tablespoon (15 ml) of cream cheese on each of the bagel halves. Press the capers into the bottom half and add the lox, red onion and dill. Top with the remaining half of the bagel and serve.

Bubbe's tip: Look, building a Jennifer is not an exact science here. Get creative and add more or less of what you want and get on with your life already. Like more cream cheese? Get schmearin'!

The Simone

Simone's ideal lox bagel. She's quite the opposite of a picky eater,
but raw onions are one thing she will flip a table over.

Prep Time: 5 minutes Cook Time: None Makes: 1 serving

2 tablespoons (30 g) Cashew Cream Cheese (page 231)

1 Bagel, Plain or Everything (page 56 or 59), sliced and toasted

3–4 chives, chopped

2 ounces (55 g) or about 3 slices Lox (page 81)

1 large slice of tomato

3–4 slices cucumber

Spread a tablespoon (15 ml) of cream cheese on each of the bagel halves. Press the chives into the bottom half and add the lox, tomato and cucumber. Top with the remaining half of the bagel and serve.

Bubbe's tip: Nobody likes a soggy bagel. Use firmer tomatoes to make your Simone as awesome as the real deal.

Traditional Egg Salad

Egg salad is a great part of a traditional Jewish spread along with bagels and whitefish salad. It's filling, yet light and perfect for any meal.

Prep Time: 5 minutes Cook Time: 20 minutes Makes: 4 servings

7 eggs

6 tablespoons (83 ml) Mayonnaise (page 228)

2 teaspoons (10 ml) organic yellow mustard

1 teaspoon dill relish

½ teaspoon onion powder

½ teaspoon salt

¼ teaspoon pepper

¼ teaspoon dried dill

In a pot that fits a steamer basket, bring a small amount of water to a boil. Put the eggs in the steamer basket and place in the pot. Cover, and allow to steam for 12 minutes.

After 12 minutes, carefully remove the basket and dunk the eggs into cold water to cool. Gently crack the eggs all over and then peel.

Chop the eggs and place in a medium-sized mixing bowl. Add the remaining ingredients and stir well.

Serve with Matzo (page 44 or 47) or scooped on top of Bibb lettuce.

Bubbe's tip: You can't break the fast without egg salad! For a perfect pairing, put a scoopala of this on a grain-free bagel or matzo. You can thank me later.

Pastured Meats and Main Courses

I hate to brag, but if my Bubbe's Brisket (page 117) isn't enough to win you the spouse of your dreams, your perfect job or a role on Broadway, then quite frankly it's you, not me. I filled this chapter with only my finest main courses like Smoky Beef Stuffed Eggplant (page 134), Roasted Leg of Lamb with Mint-Macadamia Pesto (page 125) and Balsamic Braised Short Ribs (page 122). From lamb to beef and fish to chicken, you'll have options galore. Gasp, you're looking for bacon?! You are in the wrong place my dear. But aside from split-hooved and bottom dwellers, I have got you covered from here 'til next week, and beyond.

Slow Cooker "Rotisserie" Chicken

This slow-cooked version is perfect for a labor-free weeknight meal or for a Shabbat dinner!

Prep Time: 5 minutes **Cook Time:** 4–6 hours (or overnight for Shabbat) **Makes:** 4 servings

1 whole chicken, 3–4 pounds (1.4–1.8 kg)

1 teaspoon sea salt

1 teaspoon ground black pepper

1 teaspoon paprika

½ teaspoon garlic powder

½ teaspoon onion powder

1 teaspoon salt-free all-purpose seasoning

Simply place the whole chicken into the slow cooker and sprinkle with salt, pepper, paprika, garlic powder, onion powder and all-purpose seasoning.

Cover and cook the chicken on low for 4–6 hours, or until the chicken is cooked through. The meat will fall off the bone once cooked and sliced.

Bubbe's tip: Who is ready for Shabbat dinner? Make sure you select a larger chicken and put your slow cooker on the lowest setting if cooking overnight!

Simple Roast Chicken

This method of roasting chicken may seem too simple to be true, but coating the chicken skin with salt results in crispy chicken and succulent meat. In other words, a perfect roast chicken!

Prep Time: Less than 5 minutes **Cook Time:** 75–90 minutes **Makes:** 4–6 servings, with leftovers

1 whole chicken, 3–4 pounds (1.3–1.8 kg)

1 tablespoon (15 g) finely ground sea salt

Preheat the oven to 425°F (218°C).

Pat the chicken dry with paper towels, inside and out. Coat it with salt and place in a Dutch oven (preferably) or roasting pan.

Place the pan in the oven, uncovered, and roast for 75 minutes. Check for doneness with a meat thermometer—it should reach 165°F (74°C) when stuck into the thickest part of the thigh. If it doesn't, roast for another 15 minutes, or until it comes to temperature.

Allow the chicken to rest for 10 minutes before carving.

Bubbe's tip: Oy vey, could this get any simpler? You don't even have to slaughter a backyard chicken before you cook it!

Bubbe's Brisket

This brisket comes out beautifully tender every time! Unlike barbequed brisket,
this one cooks in broth on the stovetop, which helps seal in all the juices!

Prep Time: 10 minutes Cook Time: 4 hours Makes: 4–6 servings

1 tablespoon (15 ml) avocado oil

1 teaspoon salt

Freshly ground black pepper

1 brisket, grass-fed if possible (around 4 pounds [1.8 kg])

1 large onion, sliced thin

6 large carrots, chopped

5 cloves garlic, minced

32 ounces (945 ml) Beef Broth (page 27)

Heat a large stockpot over medium-high heat and add the avocado oil.

Rub the salt and pepper into the brisket and place in the pot. Cook for about 7 minutes on each side.

Add the onion, carrots, garlic and broth to the pot. Bring to a low simmer and cover. Cook for 4 hours or until tender. Remove the brisket and allow to rest for 10 minutes.

Slice it and serve with the cooked veggies and desired greens like the Roasted Beet Salad with Pomegranate-Infused Vinaigrette (page 171).

Bubbe's tip: Us bubbes were born for brisket. It is the very meat to our potatoes. Try not to futz around with this one too much, just trust the bubbe method!

Brisket with Onions and Porcini Mushrooms

Three onions may seem like a lot, but when cooked low and slow for several hours,
they melt into the braising liquid and create a wonderful gravy.

Prep Time: 20 minutes Cook Time: 3+ hours Makes: 6–8 servings

2 ounces (55 g) dried porcini mushrooms (about 1 heaping cup)

2 cups (475 ml) boiling water

4–5 pounds (1.81–2.3 kg) brisket

1 tablespoon (15 g) salt

1 teaspoon pepper

2 tablespoons (30 ml) tallow, coconut oil, duck fat or preferred fat

2 tablespoons (30 g) tomato paste

3 large onions, sliced thin

3–4 large carrots, whole or sliced lengthwise

6 garlic cloves, peeled but left whole

12–15 fresh crimini mushrooms, whole, stemmed

Preheat the oven to 325°F (163°C).

Place the dried porcini mushrooms in a bowl and pour the boiling water over them. Let them sit for at least 15 minutes, or until you're ready to add them to the brisket.

Pat the brisket dry and season with salt and pepper.

Place a large heavy-bottomed pot over medium-high heat and melt the fat. Add the brisket and sear for 3 minutes on each side. Remove it to a plate and brush with tomato paste on both sides.

Add the onions to the pot and turn the heat to medium-low. Sauté them for 15–20 minutes, or until they're golden brown and soft.

Strain the porcini mushrooms, reserving the liquid they were in.

Once the onions are golden brown, add the carrots, then the brisket, followed by the garlic, mushrooms and the liquid from the porcini mushrooms.

Cover tightly and cook for 1½ hours. Remove the brisket to a cutting board and slice at an angle against the grain, in ¼-inch (6-mm) slices. Return back to the braising liquid, keeping them as close to the original shape of the brisket as possible. Cover and cook for an additional 1½ hours, or more if necessary, until it's tender.

Bubbe's tip: If nightshades make you meshuga, leave out the tomato paste. You can add some pureed pumpkin or sweet potato instead.

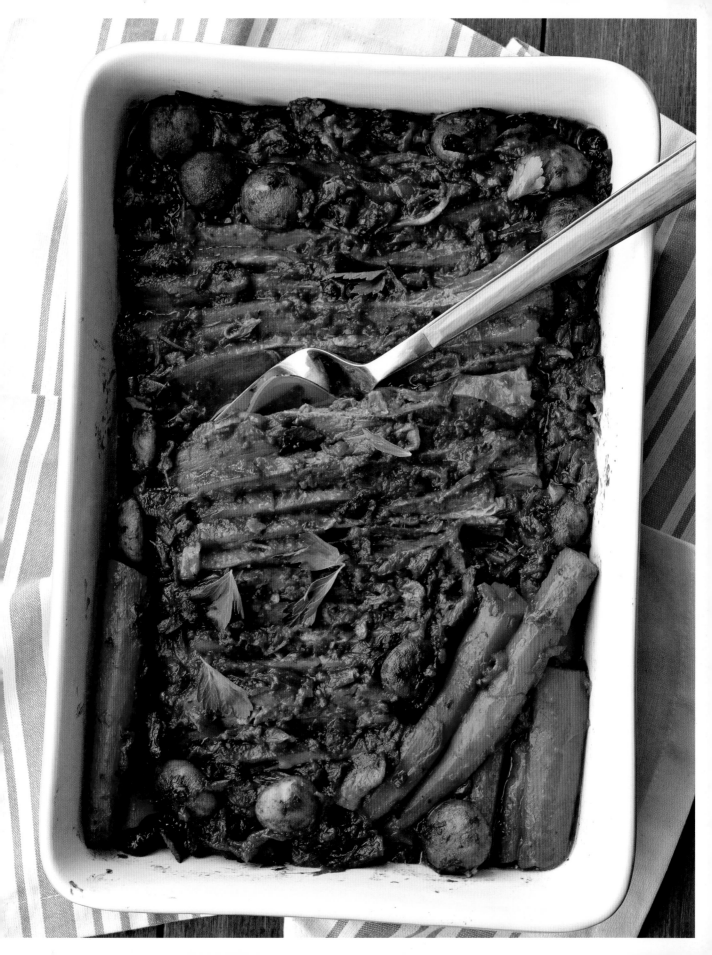

Stuffed Cabbage

Few things are as comforting as a good stuffed cabbage. This traditional Eastern European version has a sauce that is a bit sweet. If you're avoiding sugar, feel free to omit the coconut sugar.

Prep Time: 30 minutes Cook Time: 1 hour Makes: 4 servings

1 large head cabbage, preferably savoy

1 cup (150 g) finely minced onion (about 1 medium)

1 tablespoon (15 ml) light olive oil

1 teaspoon sea salt, divided

1 tablespoon (15 g) tomato paste

2 (14-ounce [397-g]) cans crushed tomatoes

½ cup (55 g) packed grated carrots (about 1 medium)

2 tablespoons (12 g) almond flour

2 eggs

1 pound (450 g) ground beef

2 tablespoons (19 g) coconut sugar

1 tablespoon (15 ml) apple cider vinegar

2 tablespoons (18 g) currants

Preheat the oven to 350°F (177°C) and bring a large pot of salted water to a boil.

Cut the core out of the bottom of the cabbage and remove as many large leaves as you can, being careful to keep them whole.

Once the water is boiling, blanch the cabbage in two batches for 3 minutes each. Remove to a bowl and allow them to cool. Once cool enough to handle, cut out the vein of each leaf.

Meanwhile, sauté the onion in a large sauce pan in the oil over medium heat until soft, about 10 minutes. Add ½ teaspoon salt, tomato paste and crushed tomatoes and simmer for 5 minutes.

In a large bowl, combine the grated carrot, almond flour, eggs, ½ teaspoon salt and beef. Once the sauce has simmered for 5 minutes, add 2 tablespoons (30 ml) of the sauce to the beef mixture and mix well with your hands to combine.

Add the coconut sugar, vinegar and currants to the sauce.

Ladle about ½ cup (120 ml) of the sauce into a small casserole dish.

Place about 2 tablespoons (30 ml) of the beef mixture into the center of each cabbage leaf and fold over the sides and roll up. Repeat with the remaining leaves and beef and place in the casserole dish. Pour the remaining sauce over the stuffed cabbage leaves.

Bake for 1 hour, uncovered. Allow the cabbage to rest for 10 minutes before serving.

Bubbe's tip: Don't waste those inner leaves! Use them for slaw. (Like the Dilly Slaw on page 163!) And if you can't have nuts, use your favorite starch as a binder in the meat mixture instead of the almond flour.

Balsamic Braised Short Ribs

There's something so decadent about short ribs, and these are certainly no exception. These are sophisticated enough to serve for a holiday dinner or special supper, but are simple enough to prepare anytime.

Prep Time: 20 minutes   Cook Time: 2½–3 hours   Makes: 4 servings

2 pounds (900 g) boneless beef short ribs

1 teaspoon salt

½ teaspoon black pepper

2 teaspoons (10 ml) avocado oil or Schmaltz (page 235)

1 large onion, large dices (about 2 cups [300 g])

3 carrots, large dices (about 1 cup [130 g])

4 stalks celery, large dices (about 1 cup [100 g])

6–8 cloves garlic, peeled

½ cup (120 ml) balsamic vinegar

1½ cups (350 ml) Chicken Broth (page 27 or 29)

1 teaspoon fish sauce

2 sprigs rosemary

4–5 sprigs thyme

Preheat the oven to 300°F (150°C). Season the short ribs on both sides with the salt and pepper.

In a Dutch oven, sear the short ribs in oil over high heat for 3 minutes on each side, or until nicely browned. Remove from the pan and set aside.

Add the onions, carrots, celery and garlic cloves to the pan, and sauté for 4–5 minutes, or until browned and beginning to soften.

Pour in the balsamic vinegar, chicken broth and fish sauce, scraping up any browned bits that have stuck to the bottom. Simmer for 1–2 minutes. Add the rosemary and thyme sprigs.

Place the short ribs back in the pot, trying to get them beneath the vegetables so they are completely submerged in the sauce and vegetables.

Cut a circle out of a piece of parchment paper, and place it over the contents of the pot and cover it with the lid.

Set the Dutch oven in the oven and roast for 2–2½ hours.

Remove the short ribs from the Dutch oven and set the pot over high heat. Boil the sauce until reduced by about half and thickened slightly, about 10 minutes. Pour the sauce back over the ribs and serve or store until the next day.

Bubbe's tip: Boneless short ribs? Oy gevalt. If using bone-in ribs like I always have, just increase the cooking time by 30 minutes, and plan about 1 pound (455 g) per person.

Roasted Leg of Lamb with Mint-Macadamia Pesto

A lot of people are intimidated by the thought of roasting a leg of lamb, but in reality, it's one of the simplest meats to prepare! Lamb is naturally so tender that marinating isn't necessary. All it needs it a simple rub of garlic and herbs.

Prep Time: 15 minutes **Cook Time:** 75–90 minutes **Makes:** 6–8 servings

5 cloves garlic, minced or pressed

2 teaspoons (10 g) salt

¼ teaspoon freshly ground black pepper

1 tablespoon (1.7 g) minced fresh rosemary

1 tablespoon (15 ml) extra virgin olive oil

1 boneless leg of lamb, about 5 pounds (2.3 kg)

1 cup (20 g) packed mint leaves

½ cup (15 g) packed parsley leaves

2 tablespoons (30 ml) lemon juice (about 1 lemon)

¼ cup (33 g) roasted salted macadamia nuts

½ teaspoon salt

½ cup (120 ml) extra virgin olive oil, more if necessary

Preheat the oven to 450°F (232°C).

In a small bowl, combine the garlic, salt, pepper, rosemary and olive oil. Untie the lamb and rub half of the paste all over the inside of the leg. Re-tie the leg and then rub the remaining paste on the outside.

Place the lamb in a roasting pan with a rack and roast at 450°F (232°C) for 15 minutes, or until it's browned on the outside.

Turn the heat down to 325°F (163°C) and cook until the internal temperature reaches 135°F (57°C) (for medium-rare), about 1 hour to 75 minutes.

Meanwhile, make the pesto by combining the mint, parsley, lemon juice, macadamia nuts, salt and oil in a blender and blend until combined. Add additional olive oil if it's too thick.

After removing the lamb from the oven, tent loosely with tin foil and allow it to rest for 10 minutes before slicing. Serve with Mint-Macadamia Pesto.

Bubbe's tip: Got extra pesto? Mix some in with Mayonnaise (page 228) for the best turkey sandwich you've ever had. Trust your bubbe!

Lemon-Coriander Grilled Lamb Chops

Tender lamb loin chops don't need long to marinate to take on great flavor.
The mix of lemon, coriander and fennel is the perfect complement for mild spring lamb.

Prep Time: 5 minutes, plus 30–60 minutes to marinate   Cook Time: 6–8 minutes   Makes: 4 servings

Zest of one lemon

3 garlic cloves, minced or pressed

1½ teaspoons (8.5 g) ground coriander

2 tablespoons (30 ml) extra virgin
olive oil

1 teaspoon lemon juice

¼ teaspoon ground fennel seeds

8 lamb loin chops, about 1½ inches
(3.8 cm) thick

In a small bowl, combine the lemon zest, garlic, coriander, olive oil, lemon juice and fennel seeds. Coat the lamb chops with the mixture and set aside for 30 minutes to 1 hour at room temperature. Refrigerate if marinating any longer than that.

Preheat the grill to medium. Once hot, grill the lamb chops for 3–4 minutes per side, for medium rare.

Bubbe's tip: You want that you should make these for a crowd and don't want to grill? Don't get verklempt! You can roast them instead for 10–12 minutes at 400°F (205°C). All right, already?

Pan-Roasted Chicken with Figs and Olives

Pan roasting chicken is a great way to get dinner on the table in less than an hour. The addition of sweet figs and salty olives adds great depth to an old favorite.

Prep Time: 15 minutes Cook Time: 45 minutes Makes: 4 servings

1 whole chicken, cut up into 8 pieces

1 teaspoon salt

¼ teaspoon black pepper

2 teaspoons (10 ml) avocado oil or Schmaltz (page 235)

1 cup (160 g) sliced shallots (about 2–3 medium)

6 dried figs, roughly chopped

1 cup (135 g) kalamata olives

1 cup (240 ml) white wine

3 sprigs thyme

Preheat the oven to 400°F (205°C) and place a large, oven-safe skillet over medium-high heat. Season the chicken all over with the salt and pepper. Add the oil to the skillet and swirl to coat. Once shimmering, add the chicken, skin side down and allow it to sear for 5–10 minutes, or until the skin is brown. Flip and cook for 2–3 minutes on the other side. Remove to a platter.

To the hot pan, add the shallots and figs and sauté for 2–3 minutes, or until the shallots are golden brown. Add the olives, wine and thyme sprigs and boil for a minute or so, scraping up any browned bits that have stuck to the bottom of the pan.

Return the chicken to the pan, skin side up and place in the oven. Roast the chicken for 30 minutes, or until it reaches an internal temperature of 165°F (74°C).

Bubbe's tip: Figs? Feh! I always made this with prunes and nobody complained. You can use either, bubula. Whatever makes you happy.

Crispy Chicken Thighs with Pomegranate Sauce

Did you know that you can get shatter-crisp chicken skin without deep frying?
Not only that, but you can have an unbelievably tasty chicken dinner on the table in 30 minutes.
You might find yourself making this one for both a dinner party and a Tuesday evening.

Prep Time: 5 minutes   Cook Time: 30–40 minutes   Makes: 4 servings

8 bone-in, skin-on chicken thighs

1½ teaspoons (9 g) kosher salt

Freshly ground black pepper

1 tablespoon (15 ml) extra virgin olive oil

1 cup (240 ml) orange juice (preferably fresh squeezed)

2 cups (450 ml) pomegranate juice

1 small sprig rosemary

2 sprigs thyme, plus more for garnish, if desired

1 teaspoon pomegranate vinegar, or red wine vinegar

2–3 tablespoons (30–45 ml) pomegranate arils

Season the chicken on both sides with salt and pepper.

Heat the olive oil in a large skillet over medium heat and add the chicken, skin side down. Allow it to cook for 20–25 minutes, until the skin is deep golden brown. Make sure not to move it for at least the first 10 minutes, or the skin might stick to the pan. After that, rotate the chicken and/or the pan to get all of the pieces browned evenly, but trying to move them as little as possible. Once they are evenly golden brown, flip and cook for an additional 10–15 minutes, or until they are fully cooked and reach an internal temperature of 165°F (74°C).

Meanwhile, place the orange juice, pomegranate juice, rosemary and thyme in a medium sauce pan and bring to a boil. Allow the mixture to boil until reduced to about ½ cup (120 ml), about 15–25 minutes. Strain the herbs and stir in the vinegar.

Serve the chicken over the sauce, garnished with pomegranate arils and fresh thyme, if desired.

Bubbe's tip: The chicken skin won't get crispy if you futz with it! Put down the tongs, bubula. If you need something to do, knit a sweater.

Savory Lamb Goulash

If you prefer a little more culinary excitement than beef and chicken, this lamb goulash is for you.
It is savory and packed with flavor, yet is family friendly without being too sophisticated.
The smoked paprika really adds personality to this delicious dish!

Prep Time: 10 minutes Cook Time: 45 minutes Makes: 6 servings

1 bell pepper, seeded and diced

2 Yukon gold potatoes, diced

1 cup (130 g) carrots, diced

1 onion, diced

3 tablespoons (45 ml) olive oil, avocado oil or preferred cooking fat

1 pound (450 g) pasture-raised lamb, ground

1½ cups (270 g) diced tomatoes

1 cup (240 ml) Beef Broth (page 27)

1 teaspoon garlic powder

1 teaspoon cumin

1 teaspoon smoked paprika

½ teaspoon turmeric

2 teaspoons (5 g) paprika

¼ teaspoon ground black pepper

Flat leaf parsley to garnish

Begin by sautéing the bell pepper, potatoes, carrots and onion in the cooking fat over medium heat until the vegetables are softened and fork tender, about 10 minutes.

Add in the ground lamb and continue cooking, breaking apart with a spoon to make it crumbled as it cooks. Add in the tomatoes, broth, garlic powder, cumin, smoked paprika, turmeric, paprika and black pepper and bring to a simmer over medium heat.

Cover and allow it to cook for 20 minutes. Remove the lid and check the consistency; it should be thick and hearty like a stew. If it is too soupy, allow it to cook for 5 more minutes uncovered over medium heat, stirring to prevent burning. If it is too thick, add a bit more broth.

Serve topped with flat leaf parsley to garnish.

Note: If making for Shabbat dinner, simply cook the lamb over high heat in a medium-sized skillet, transfer to a slow cooker, add remaining ingredients and cook on low overnight as needed to observe the kosher laws.

Bubbe's tip: Stretch your gelt with this recipe!! If you want to feed more mouths, add in extra veggies and keep costs down. How's that for using your noodle (kugel)??

Smoky Beef–Stuffed Eggplant

This dish is as beautiful as it is savory. Eggplants stuffed with a smoky beef mixture, topped with chopped pistachios make for an extraordinary meal that takes minimal effort!

Prep Time: 15 minutes Cook Time: 1½ hours Makes: 4 servings

FOR THE EGGPLANTS
2 eggplants sliced lengthwise

2 tablespoons (30 ml) avocado oil or olive oil

Sea salt and pepper

FOR THE BEEF MIXTURE
2 teaspoons (10 ml) avocado oil or olive oil

1 onion, diced

1 pound (450 g) organic, grass-fed ground beef

¼ teaspoon smoked paprika

½ teaspoon sea salt

4 cloves garlic, minced

½ teaspoon onion powder

1 teaspoon parsley, chopped

⅓ cup (55 g) diced tomatoes

FOR THE SAUCE
⅓ cup (80 ml) crushed tomatoes

1 tablespoon (15 ml) maple syrup

¼ teaspoon onion powder

¼ teaspoon smoked paprika

¼ teaspoon garlic powder

Pinch sea salt

TO GARNISH
¼ cup (35 g) chopped pistachios

Flat leaf parsley

Preheat the oven to 400°F (205°C). Score the fleshy side of the eggplants vertically and horizontally and baste the same side with the oil. Season with sea salt and pepper and arrange them skin side up in a casserole dish. Slide the dish into the oven and bake for 20 minutes.

Meanwhile, heat a large pan over medium-high heat and add the oil. Once the oil is shimmering add the onion and beef, along with the paprika, salt, garlic, onion powder and parsley. Sauté for 8–10 minutes, or until the beef is cooked. Add the diced tomatoes and cook 5 minutes more.

In a separate saucepan, bring the sauce ingredients to a simmer over high heat, stirring occasionally. Allow the sauce to simmer for 5–8 minutes and then remove from the heat.

Once the eggplants are finished baking, remove them from the oven, flip them fleshy side up and spoon the meat mixture into them. Reduce the heat to 375°F (190°C). Use a spoon to help press the meat into the scored flesh. Cover the casserole dish with foil and return them, open-faced, to the oven for 45 minutes.

After 45 minutes has passed, remove the casserole dish from the oven, take off the foil and top the meat with the sauce, evenly distributing it among the four eggplant halves. Then, return them uncovered to the oven for 15 final minutes of cooking.

Remove the casserole dish one last time, top the eggplants with the chopped pistachios and parsley and serve hot.

Bubbe's tip: If you are as saucy as I am, you might want to double the smoky tomato sauce for this recipe. Trust me bubula, I did not earn bubbe status overnight for nothing.

Shakshuka

This classic Israeli breakfast is wonderful for dinner, too. With poached eggs and savory tomato sauce seasoned with cumin and smoked paprika, it's as gorgeous as it is delicious. And who doesn't love a one-pot meal?

Prep Time: 10 minutes Cook Time: 35–40 minutes Makes: 4–6 servings

3 tablespoons (45 ml) extra virgin olive oil, divided

1 small onion, cut into small dices

3 cloves garlic, sliced

2 bell peppers, cut into small dices

1 teaspoon smoked paprika

½ teaspoon ground cumin

½ teaspoon ground coriander

½ teaspoon turmeric

¼ teaspoon cayenne

1 tablespoon (15 g) tomato paste

½ teaspoon salt

28 ounces (795 g) diced tomatoes, or 2 pounds (900 g) fresh

4–6 eggs

Heat a large skillet over medium heat and add 2 tablespoons (30 ml) of the olive oil. Once shimmering, add the onions and sauté for 8–10 minutes, stirring occasionally, until they are golden brown and softened.

Add the garlic and peppers and sauté for another 3–4 minutes, until the garlic is golden brown.

Add the spices and stir constantly for a minute, or until very fragrant, being careful not to let them burn.

Add the tomato paste and stir into the vegetables, cooking until it's a brick red color, about 30 seconds to 1 minute.

Add the salt and diced tomatoes and stir, scraping up any browned bits that have stuck to the bottom.

Bring to a simmer and cook for 10 minutes, stirring occasionally.

Turn off the heat and make four to six indentations in the sauce and crack the eggs into them. Turn the heat back on so it's at a gentle simmer and allow the eggs to cook for 8 minutes.

Cover and cook for an additional 3–5 minutes, or until the eggs are cooked to your liking. Drizzle with the remaining olive oil.

Bubbe's tip: Bubula, you need to eat your vegetables! Serve this with a salad on the side, or throw in a handful of spinach or watercress during the last 10 minutes, before adding the eggs. Was that so difficult?

Mustard and Chive Fish Cakes

Fish latkes?! Well, not exactly. But these fish cakes come together just as easily and are perfect for weeknight meals, while being much more interesting than steamed fish and veggies.

Prep Time: 20 minutes   Cook Time: 35 minutes   Makes: 4 servings

24 ounces (680 g) white fish (cod, tilapia, haddock)

4 tablespoons (6 g) fresh chives, minced

1 onion, diced

1 teaspoon sea salt

2 teaspoons (10 ml) Dijon mustard

3 cloves garlic, minced

½ teaspoon dill, dried or fresh, minced

1 tablespoon (15 ml) coconut aminos

1 egg

½ cup (65 g) arrowroot flour

2 tablespoons (30 ml) avocado oil or olive oil

Preheat the oven to 350°F (177°C). Finely mince your fish into small pieces; they do not need to be uniform in size, but should be small in size so that the fish cakes come together easily.

Using a towel, squeeze any excess water out of the fish, especially if it has been frozen and thawed. Next, combine the minced fish with all remaining ingredients, except the cooking oil, in a mixing bowl, using your hands to incorporate well.

Then, form your fish cakes by firmly pressing together the fish mixture into palm-sized patties. Place them on a parchment-lined baking sheet and bake them for 20 minutes. During the last 5 minutes of bake time, heat the cooking oil in a large skillet over high heat.

Carefully remove the baking sheet from the oven and using a thin, flexible spatula, transfer one fish cake to the hot oil. Cook for up to 4 minutes on each side or until they are nicely browned. Repeat with remaining fish cakes, being careful not to overcrowd the skillet. Serve warm.

Note: To make a tasty aioli to top your fish cakes, simply squeeze some fresh lemon juice and dijon mustard into Mayonnaise (page 228) and stir in your favorite herbs.

Bubbe's tip: Look, I know you are more than just another shayna punim—so use that head of yours and make sure you squeeze all that water out of your fish. Otherwise, don't get all bent when your fish cakes are more like fish soup!!!

Israeli Fish Stew

While fish stew might not necessarily conjure up childhood memories of your bubbe in the kitchen (or maybe it does), it is a simple and flavorful way of putting dinner on the table. The rich stock and wild-caught fish in this zesty dish come together beautifully!

Prep Time: 10 minutes Cook Time: 40 minutes Makes: 4 servings

1 tablespoon (15 ml) avocado or olive oil

1 large onion, diced

5 plum tomatoes, seeded and diced

1 tablespoon (15 g) tomato paste

3 cloves garlic, minced

8 ounces (240 ml) Chicken Broth (page 27 or 28)

1½ pounds (680 g) white fish (like cod), cut into chunks

½ teaspoon paprika

¼ teaspoon black pepper

1 teaspoon cumin

Pinch turmeric

½ teaspoon ground ginger

Sea salt to taste

Fresh cilantro leaves and toasted almond slivers for garnishing, optional

Heat a large skillet over medium heat. Add the oil. Once shimmering, add the onion and sauté until golden brown and softened, about 8–10 minutes. Add in the tomatoes, tomato paste, garlic and chicken broth and bring to a simmer.

Once simmering, add the fish and remaining seasonings. Stir gently to combine. Cover the simmering mixture, turn the heat to low and cook for 10 minutes until the fish is cooked through.

Remove the lid for the last 5 minutes so that excess liquid can evaporate and a stew-like texture is achieved. Serve hot, garnished with fresh cilantro leaves and toasted almond slivers, if desired.

Bubbe's tip: Don't skimp on the garnishes!! The cilantro and toasted almonds provide texture, color and flavor!

Cholent

Cholent, in many Yiddish kitchens, is the main Sabbath meal; a slow-cooked combination of tender beef, vegetables and, traditionally, beans. When observing Sabbath, the day of rest includes no cooking, so a slowly cooked meal (either on the stovetop or slow cooker) allows for proper adherence to this law. In this recipe, the beans are omitted to keep it legume-free. Carrots and potatoes help to make it a filling and satisfying dish.

Prep Time: 10 minutes Cook Time: 8–18 hours, depending on whether served for Shabbat Makes: 4–5 servings

2 pounds (900 g) grass-fed brisket or beef spare ribs

5 Yukon Gold potatoes, diced

1 cup (130 g) chopped carrots

1 onion, diced

1 cup (165 g) diced tomatoes

2 cups (475 ml) Beef Broth (page 27)

1 teaspoon sea salt

½ teaspoon paprika

½ teaspoon smoked paprika

½ teaspoon ground black pepper

Using your slow cooker, place all ingredients inside and set on the lowest setting. If observing Shabbat, cook overnight until ready to serve for dinner (over 12 hours).

If you are preparing for any other meal you may cook on high for up to 8 hours or on low for 8–10 hours, until the meat is tender and cooked through. The brisket should pull apart easily and be fork tender.

Bubbe's tip: What, no beans?! No barley?! What kind of cholent is this?! This cholent is made both legume- and grain-free so you can forego the bloating and discomfort. You'll thank me later, bubula!

Garden-Fresh Salads and Veggies

Look, I don't want to get all meshuga, but if you don't eat your veggies, you certainly aren't going to be strong and healthy like I am in your old age. What, you think I got this gorgeous eating Chocolate Babka for every meal?! Let's be honest here. I've written these recipes so that if you don't like veggies so much, you will love them by the end of this chapter. The Savory Sautéed Veggie Kugel (page 160) may become your new favorite; or maybe even the Ginger-Lime Beet and Apple Salad (page 172). Plus, I've included three kinds of latkes so you can sneak in more veggies by frying them in schmaltz. It's what nature intended. L'chaim!

Field Greens with Pomegranate Seeds and Maple Vinaigrette

This colorful salad is so vibrant it's hard to believe it's straight from nature! The iconic pomegranate seeds, a Jewish symbol, add a hint of sweet while the warmth of the roasted pecans brings an earthy balance.

Prep Time: 15 minutes Cook Time: None Makes: 4–5 servings

7 ounces (200 g) mixed field greens

4 ounces (115 g) pomegranate seeds

4 ounces (115 g) pecan halves or pieces, roasted and salted

½ cup (120 ml) olive oil

¼ cup (60 ml) avocado oil

¼ cup (60 ml) red wine vinegar

½ teaspoon dry mustard

2 garlic cloves, minced

¼ teaspoon black pepper, ground

¼ teaspoon sea salt

1 tablespoon (15 ml) maple syrup

1 teaspoon dried parsley

Juice from ½ lemon

In a large serving bowl, place the greens in the bottom, followed by the pomegranate seeds and then topped with the roasted pecans.

Next make the maple vinaigrette by combining the remaining ingredients in a cruet and shaking well to combine thoroughly.

Once ready to serve, drizzle the desired amount of dressing over the greens and toss to mix ingredients. You'll have dressing leftover, which can be refrigerated until ready to use.

Bubbe's tip: Oy vey, the nut allergies! If the pecans are a problem, substitute sunflower seeds. All right, already?!

Braised Purple Cabbage

Pickled, fermented, braised or shredded, purple cabbage is easy on the eyes and delicious on the taste buds. This side dish makes a perfect companion to Bubbe's Brisket (page 117) or Balsamic Braised Short Ribs (page 122).

Prep Time: 10 minutes Cook Time: 30 minutes Makes: 6 servings

3 tablespoons (45 ml) avocado oil, olive oil or preferred cooking fat

1 head purple cabbage, chopped

½ onion, diced

4 garlic cloves, minced

1 cup (240 ml) Chicken Broth (page 27 or 28)

1 tablespoon (15 ml) apple cider vinegar

1 teaspoon sea salt

½ teaspoon ground black pepper

Heat a large skillet over medium-high heat. Add the oil. Once shimmering, add the cabbage and onion.

After about 5 minutes, add in all the garlic, chicken broth, vinegar, salt and pepper. Cover and cook for 15 minutes, checking periodically. For the last bit of cook time, about 5–10 minutes, remove the lid and allow any excess liquid to cook off. Serve warm.

Bubbe's tip: What?! Purple cabbage gives you anxiety? Any color cabbage will work. Relax bubula, don't stress that kop of yours.

Tzimmes

Tzimmes, which literally means a great fuss or uproar, is also a delicious dish that gives you the freedom to personalize your favorite root veggies and then cast a sweet or savory tone. This one uses a bit of honey and orange, mixed with garlic and sea salt, for a perfect balance.

Prep Time: 10 minutes **Cook Time:** 2 hours **Makes:** 4 servings

2 pounds (900 g) rainbow carrots (about 10 carrots)

1 orange, juiced

8 ounces (240 ml) Chicken Broth (page 27 or 28)

½ teaspoon onion powder

2 cloves garlic, minced

2 tablespoons (30 ml) honey

½ teaspoon sea salt

3 tablespoons (45 ml) olive oil

¼ teaspoon ground black pepper

½ cup (60 g) dried cranberries, optional

Preheat the oven to 350°F (177°C).

Clean, peel and coarsely chop the rainbow carrots. If you cannot find rainbow carrots, regular orange carrots will work too.

In a mixing bowl combine orange juice, broth, onion powder, garlic, honey, sea salt, olive oil and black pepper.

In a casserole dish, place chopped carrots on the bottom and then pour the broth mixture over the top.

If desired, you can now add in cranberries. Cover with a lid, or foil, and bake for 2 hours.

Bubbe's tip: Don't make a tzimmes! If you are too busy, toss the ingredients into a slow cooker and let them cook on low for about 4 hours.

Sweet Potato Latkes

If nightshades are problematic, these sweet potato latkes are the perfect substitution. This naturally sweet starch is delicious paired with garlic and onion and fries up beautifully for a white potato stand-in!

Prep Time: 10 minutes Cook Time: 30 minutes Makes: 4 servings

Avocado oil, Schmaltz (page 235) or preferred cooking fat for frying

1 medium sweet potato, sliced with a spiral slicer and diced (or grated)

1 medium sweet potato, cooked and mashed

½ onion, minced

2 eggs

½ cup (60 g) tapioca starch

1 teaspoon onion powder

1 teaspoon garlic powder

1 teaspoon sea salt

½ teaspoon ground black pepper

Preheat enough oil to cover the bottom of a large, deep skillet over medium-high heat. Combine all the remaining ingredients in a bowl and mix thoroughly until all ingredients are incorporated.

Once the oil is glistening (hot enough for frying), drop large spoonsful into the oil and slightly flatten them with the back of a spoon.

Using a thin, flexible spatula, flip each latke over once the underneath side is nicely browned, about 4 minutes. Watch to make sure the oil isn't too hot or they can burn quickly.

Likewise, oil that is not hot enough will leave the latkes greasy.

Once both sides are browned, remove the latkes from the oil and place them on a towel-lined plate. Repeat as necessary, frying in small batches.

Note: If you are using grated sweet potato, make sure to use a towel and really press out as much moisture as you can from the sweet potato shreds. They will not fry well if this step is omitted.

Bubbe's tip: Cooking for the whole mishpocheh? Keep these cooked batches in a warm oven while you fry the rest. No one likes a cold latke!

Latkes

"Are white potatoes Paleo?" has been quite the heated debate over the years. We say the answer is yes! While they may not be the most nutrient-dense food out there, they are a whole food and perfectly acceptable to include in most diets. And boy, do they make a mean latke!

Prep Time: 10 minutes + 1 hour to sweat the potatoes Cook Time: 30 minutes Makes: 3 dozen, 3-inch (7.5-cm) latkes

5 pounds (2.3 kg) russet potatoes, peeled or scrubbed

1 large (¾ pound [340 g]) onion

1 tablespoon (15 g) salt

4 eggs

1 cup (140 g) potato starch

2 cups (475 ml) fat for frying; duck fat being the #1 choice, or you can use light olive oil

Grate the potato and onion with the shredder blade of your food processor or with a box grater.

Place the shredded potato and onion in a large colander and with your hands, mix in the tablespoon (15 g) of salt. Place either in the sink, or over a large bowl. The potatoes and onion will release a lot of liquid.

In a large bowl, beat together the eggs and potato starch.

After about an hour, squeeze as much liquid as you can out of the potatoes and onion and add to the bowl with the eggs and potato starch. Mix well. (Again, your hands are probably the best tools, here.)

In a large skillet, heat 1 cup (240 ml) of the oil over medium heat. To test if it's hot enough, drop in a shred of potato. It should sizzle right away. Once the oil is hot enough, drop quarter cupfuls (60 ml) of the potato mixture into the pan and flatten into a pancake shape. Press down with the back of a metal spatula to flatten further. This will also help them bind.

Fry for 4–5 minutes, or until the edges are brown. Flip and cook for another 2–3 minutes, or until golden brown.

Add more oil as needed and make sure you let it get hot again before adding another batch of latkes.

Transfer finished latkes to drain on several layers of paper towels. Putting a paper bag underneath the paper towels will allow you to use less of them.

If eating right away, keep in a warm oven until they're all ready to eat. Alternately, freeze of refrigerate until ready to eat.

To reheat, bake the latkes in a single layer at 450°F (232°C) for 5–7 minutes, or until sizzling hot.

Bubbe's tip: Don't have potato starch in the pantry? Don't plotz! Do this: Put a large bowl under the colander of potatoes to catch the liquid that drains out. After an hour, pour off the liquid and gather up the starch that has gathered at the bottom of the bowl. Mix that into your batter with the other ingredients, and you're ready to latke!

Carrot Parsnip Latkes

Everyone loves latkes! These savory, vegetable pancakes are a nice switch from the traditional white potato variety. By adding in parsnips and carrots, you'll find a different flavor element from potatoes. Yet, you'll love serving them up with Horseradish Sour Cream (page 224), just as you would the original recipe!

Prep Time: 10 minutes **Cook Time:** 30 minutes **Makes:** About 20 latkes

3 large parsnips, about 1 pound (450 g)

4 medium carrots, about ½ pound (230 g)

3 eggs

¼ cup (30 g) tapioca starch

¼ cup (12 g) minced chives

1 teaspoon salt

Oil for frying, about 1 cup (240 ml)

Either with a box grater or the grater attachment of your food processor, grate the parsnips and carrots. In a large bowl, mix them with the eggs, tapioca, chives and salt.

Heat a large skillet over medium-high heat. Add about a third of the oil and heat until it shimmers.

Drop the pancake mixture into the pan, about ¼ cup (60 ml) each, and flatten into a pancake shape. Allow the latkes to cook for 2–3 minutes, or until deep golden brown. Flip and cook an additional 2–3 minutes, until cooked through. Adjust your heat between medium and medium-high as needed. Remove cooked pancakes to several layers of paper towels.

Repeat with the remaining mixture, adding more oil as needed in between batches.

Bubbe's tip: Bubula, make sure you're wearing an apron when frying these. The oil might splatter! Better it splashes on a verkakte apron than a nice blouse!

Sweet Potato Kugel

When egg noodles are out, as with a grain-free lifestyle, this Sweet Potato Kugel is the perfect stand-in. It is truly reminiscent of the old favorite, but, with spiral cut sweet potatoes, takes a much healthier approach!

Prep Time: 10 minutes Cook Time: 40 minutes Makes: 8 servings

2 large sweet potatoes, peeled and cut into ribbons or noodles with a spiral slicer or vegetable peeler

3 tablespoons (45 ml) olive oil, plus more for greasing the pan

5 eggs

1 cup (240 ml) full-fat coconut milk

⅓ cup (80 g) coconut palm sugar

½ teaspoon sea salt

1 teaspoon ground cinnamon

Preheat the oven to 375°F (190°C). Grease an 8 x 8 inch (20 x 20 cm) casserole dish. Then, in a skillet, heat the sweet potato in the olive oil over medium heat for about 6–8 minutes, or until the sweet potato softens.

While the sweet potato is cooking, mix all the remaining ingredients in a mixing bowl, stirring to combine well. Once the sweet potatoes are ready, remove them from the heat and incorporate into the egg mixture.

Next, pour the mix into the prepared casserole dish and bake for about 30–40 minutes, or until an inserted toothpick comes out clean. Slice and serve warm.

Bubbe's tip: Use your "noodle"! Experiment with different sizes of spiral sliced sweet potato. You can make them wide and flat like egg noodles or long and thin like spaghetti.

Savory Sautéed Veggie Kugel

Most people think of kugels as being slightly sweet with egg noodles, cinnamon and lots of dairy. While that is one tasty preparation, there are certainly others! This one packs in lots of veggies and is perfect for a side dish, yet hearty enough for a meal. Take your pick!

Prep Time: 20 minutes Cook Time: 1 hour Makes: 6 servings

2 tablespoons (30 ml) olive oil

1 zucchini, shredded or julienned

1 large sweet potato, shredded or julienned

1 cup (115 g) shredded rainbow carrots

1 onion, diced

1 teaspoon sea salt

½ teaspoon garlic powder

½ teaspoon onion powder

½ teaspoon ground black pepper

3 eggs

1 cup (30 g) baby spinach, chopped

1 tablespoon (3 g) fresh or dried chives, minced

3 tablespoons (18 g) almond flour

Preheat the oven to 350°F (177°C). In a large skillet over medium-high heat, drizzle the olive oil. Add the zucchini, sweet potato, carrots, onion, salt, garlic powder, onion powder and black pepper to the skillet.

Sauté the ingredients on medium-high for 10–15 minutes, shifting the vegetables regularly so that they do not burn. You want them to soften and for any excess moisture to evaporate prior to baking. Turn the heat to high if there is residual liquid in the pan. After the vegetables are cooked and starting to brown slightly, remove them from heat, allowing them to cool for a few minutes so that they do not cook the eggs.

Once slightly cooled, add the eggs one at a time and stir into the vegetable mixture. Then add the spinach, chives and almond flour. Once combined thoroughly, pour mixture into a greased, 8 x 6 inch (20 x 15 cm) casserole dish. You may use a larger casserole dish, but you'll need to adjust baking time accordingly.

Now bake the mixture, uncovered for around 45 minutes, or until the center is set. If you choose to use a larger casserole dish, you may need less baking time. Allow the kugel to cool slightly before slicing into squares and serving.

Bubbe's tip: Have another favorite veggie? Let your hair down, why not?! Add in a variety of other plants to customize your kugel. I won't tell anyone, you rule-breaker!

Dilly Slaw

A good slaw is a deli staple and is also a great side dish for chicken or brisket.
This one is tangy, creamy and spiked with fresh dill.

Prep Time: 20 minutes Cook Time: None Makes: 6–8 servings

¼ cup (60 ml) apple cider vinegar

2 tablespoons (30 ml) honey

¼ cup (60 ml) Mayonnaise (page 228)

¼ cup (2 g) minced dill

¼ teaspoon celery seed

1 medium head cabbage, shredded
(about 8 cups [560 g])

2 large carrots, shredded (about 2 cups
[220 g])

¼ large red onion, sliced thin

In a large bowl, combine the apple cider vinegar, honey, mayonnaise, dill and celery seed. Stir to combine.

Add in the cabbage, carrots and red onion. Using either a gloved or clean hand, mix to combine, squeezing the veggies while you stir. Serve chilled.

Bubbe's tip: Don't like dill? No need to kvetch about it! Just use another herb instead. Or just leave it out! It will still be delicious.

Israeli Salad

This delicious classic is perfect for any occasion. It is a refreshing and nutrient-dense, plant-based side that can easily be made a meal if you introduce a bit of protein.

Prep Time: 15 minutes Cook Time: None Makes: 6 servings

5 Roma tomatoes, seeded and diced small

3 Persian cucumbers, diced small

½ small onion, diced small

1 small handful minced fresh parsley

2 garlic cloves, minced

1 tablespoon (15 ml) olive oil

Juice from 1 lemon

Sea salt and ground black pepper to taste

¼ cup (30 g) toasted pine nuts, optional

Combine all ingredients and toss together. Keep refrigerated until ready to serve. If adding in the pine nuts, you'll want to add them in just before serving so they remain fresh and crunchy.

Bubbe's tip: Oh what, you want more excitement in your life? How about you add in some diced avocado and quit with the whining!

Tabbouleh

Tabbouleh typically involves bulgur wheat, which you will not find here!
Instead we've used finely chopped cashews for even more flavor and texture.

Prep Time: 15 minutes Cook Time: None Makes: 4 servings

3 cups (120 g) flat leaf parsley, finely chopped

3 Roma tomatoes, seeded and finely diced

2 green onions, finely minced

⅓ cup (37 g) roasted and salted finely chopped cashews

1 lemon, juiced

1 tablespoon (15 ml) avocado or extra virgin olive oil

Black pepper to taste

Sea salt to taste

Combine parsley, diced tomatoes, green onions and cashews in a mixing bowl and toss. Next, squeeze the lemon juice and drizzle the oil, toss again and season with salt and pepper to taste. Serve chilled.

Bubbe's tip: Are nuts a pain in your tuches? Good news—you can leave them out and substitute ground sunflower seeds instead. Problem solved!

Pan-Fried Brussels Sprouts with Cranberries and Pine Nuts

Remember when Brussels sprouts were pushed off the table and fed to the dog? No more! These are so full of flavor you'd never imagine they were ever banned from dinner.

Prep Time: 10 minutes Cook Time: 15 minutes Makes: 4 servings

12 ounces (340 g) Brussels sprouts

2 tablespoons (30 ml) avocado or extra virgin olive oil

½ onion, diced

½ teaspoon garlic powder

½ teaspoon sea salt (or more to taste)

¼ teaspoon ground black pepper

¼ cup (30 g) dried cranberries

¼ cup (30 g) pine nuts

Begin by trimming and halving the Brussels sprouts. In a large skillet, drizzle the cooking oil over high heat and then introduce the Brussels sprouts and diced onion.

Season with the garlic powder, sea salt and ground black pepper and cook for around 10 minutes, shifting the contents so they do not burn.

For the last 5 minutes of cook time, add in the cranberries and pine nuts. Stir so that the pine nuts toast but do not burn. Serve warm.

Bubbe's tip: Don't know how to pair your Brussels? These are perfect with the Roast Chicken (page 114) or even my own Bubbe's Brisket (page 117). Get cooking already, would ya!

Roasted Beet Salad
with Pomegranate-Infused Vinaigrette

This is a beautiful salad that will entertain your eyes as much as your palate;
and the pomegranate infused vinaigrette is perfectly paired with the earthy beets.

Prep Time: 15 minutes Cook Time: 15 minutes Makes: 4 servings

FOR THE SALAD

2 golden beets, cleaned and peeled

2 red beets, cleaned and peeled

2 tablespoons (30 ml) olive oil

Sea salt + black pepper to taste

5 ounces (140 g) mixed field greens

FOR THE VINAIGRETTE

2 tablespoons (30 ml) honey

1 teaspoon Dijon mustard

⅓ cup (80 ml) avocado or olive oil

⅓ cup + 1 tablespoon (95 ml)
pomegranate-infused red wine vinegar

¼ teaspoon onion powder

¼ teaspoon garlic powder

¼ teaspoon sea salt (or more to taste)

FOR THE GARNISH

¼ cup (16 g) toasted and salted
pumpkin seeds (or more to taste)

Preheat the oven to 425°F (218°C). Slice the beets as thin as possible or use a mandolin and slice about ⅛-inch (3-mm) thick. Place the beet slices in a casserole dish.

Baste the slices with the olive oil and then season with salt and pepper to taste. Bake for 15 minutes. Then, carefully remove from the oven and allow them to cool.

While the beets are roasting, mix all the vinaigrette ingredients in a cruet or jar and shake to combine. Refrigerate until ready to use.

Combine the roasted beets with the field greens and top with toasted pumpkin seeds. Drizzle the pomegranate-infused vinaigrette as desired.

Bubbe's tip: I don't want to brag, but you will want to keep this vinaigrette on hand for every day of the year. Now listen to your bubbe, will you?

Ginger-Lime Beet and Apple Salad

This salad may only have a handful of ingredients, but it's packed full of flavor. The ginger and lime are the perfectly bright complement to the earthy beets. It's wonderful with a Simple Roast Chicken (page 114).

Prep Time: 15 minutes Cook Time: None Makes: 4 servings

6 small beets, about ½ pound (230 g) or 1 bunch, peeled

1 medium green apple

2 teaspoons (4 g) grated fresh ginger

3 tablespoons (45 ml) lime juice

3 tablespoons (45 ml) extra virgin olive oil

¼ teaspoon salt

Grate the beets and apple with the coarse side of a box grater or with the grater attachment of your food processor.

In a large bowl, combine the beet and apple with remaining ingredients and stir to combine.

Bubbe's tip: This salad packs the most punch when it's first made. If you want to make it ahead, keep the dressing separate and mix together shortly before serving.

Honey Dijon Asparagus

Asparagus might possibly be the easiest vegetable to prep and cook, and this simple recipe doesn't complicate things. It's great warm or cold, making it a great side dish to make ahead for Shabbat.

Prep Time: 5 minutes Cook Time: 2–4 minutes Makes: 4 servings

Water for boiling
2 teaspoons (10 ml) white wine vinegar
1 teaspoon honey
1 tablespoon (15 ml) Dijon mustard
½ teaspoon fresh tarragon or dill, minced
1 tablespoon (15 g) salt
1 pound (450 g) asparagus

Make sure you have a clean kitchen towel handy, and bring a medium pot of water to a boil.

In a large bowl, combine the white wine vinegar, honey, Dijon mustard and fresh tarragon.

Add the salt and asparagus to the boiling water and blanch for 2–4 minutes, depending on the thickness of your asparagus and how soft you prefer it.

Once cooked to your desired tenderness, remove asparagus with tongs to the clean kitchen towel. Arrange in as much as a single layer as possible to allow the asparagus to cool.

After about a minute, toss the asparagus with the prepared dressing. Serve either warm or chilled.

Bubbe's tip: If your asparagus are extra thick, you should peel the ends with a vegetable peeler. What? You're so busy?

Naturally Sweetened Treats

Let me guess, you've been waiting to get to this chapter. Trust me, I know. Our people love the carbs and have never met a blintz they didn't like. Oh wait, except for those ones at Morty's house that one time—that was a disaster on a plate. But you catch my drift, don't you, bubula? We love starches more than our first-born. In fact, we love them so much we are even willing to eat them unleavened! Now, if you didn't notice, those traditional delights are typically made with wheat flour, which is basically verkakte, especially for those who are intolerant. I've baked you all your favorites from Hamantaschen (page 179) to Honey Cake (page 192) and from Babka (page 195) to Macaroons (pages 199 and 200). What, you want donut holes for Hanukkah? How about two of them to choose from, including chocolate and jelly! I want that you should enjoy your treats without the bloat and discomfort. You can thank me later. You're welcome.

Hamantaschen

These triangular, hat-shaped cookies are a childhood (and adulthood) favorite! Here are two options for fillings, raspberry and apricot, though there are endless possibilities!

Prep Time: 20 minutes Cook Time: 10 minutes Makes: 6 servings

FOR THE COOKIE
1 cup (110 g) cashews

1 egg

1 cup (95 g) almond flour

Pinch sea salt

½ teaspoon baking soda

3 tablespoons (45 ml) maple syrup

¼ cup (28 g) coconut flour

FOR THE BERRY FILLING
1 cup (140 g) frozen raspberries (or fresh, if in season)

¼ cup (60 g) coconut palm sugar

½ lemon, juiced

FOR THE APRICOT FILLING
½ cup (160 g) fruit-sweetened apricot preserves

1 tablespoon (8 g) poppy seeds

Bubbe's tip: Want to try other flavors? The world is your Hamantaschen… try chocolate or even prunes for variety!

Preheat the oven to 350°F (177°C). To make the cookies, place the cashews into a food processor or blender and pulse until you have a "flour." Next add in egg, almond flour, salt, baking soda and maple syrup. Blend more until all ingredients are well combined and form a dough.

Spoon the dough onto a piece of parchment paper and begin sprinkling in the coconut flour, 1 tablespoon (7 g) at a time. The dough will be sticky to start, but the coconut flour will take care of this.

Once the stickiness is gone, roll out the dough between two pieces of parchment paper until it is about ¼-inch (6-mm) thick. Use a drinking glass or round cookie cutter (with a 3-inch [7.5-cm] diameter) to cut circles out of the dough. Set the circles aside.

To make the berry filling—which can also be made ahead if you prefer—combine the raspberries, sugar and lemon juice in a small saucepan over medium heat. Then mash the fruit until it is soft and combines well with the sugar. Allow the mixture to simmer for about 8 minutes or until it thickens and reduces. If there are any residual lumps you may briefly puree until a smoother consistency is achieved.

Alternatively, to make the apricot filling, combine the preserves with the poppy seeds and stir well.

Next, continue to assemble the cookies by taking one dough circle and placing a dollop of the raspberry filling in the center, no more than ½ teaspoon or so; do not overfill.

Then fold the circle into thirds, sealing off the edges until a triangular shape is formed. Make sure you pinch the seams closed, or they can reopen while baking.

Repeat until all of the dough is used. Place cookies on a parchment-lined baking sheet and bake for 10 minutes. Remove from the oven and allow to cool slightly before serving.

Rugelach

Is rugelach the official Jewish cookie? It very well could be. If neither of the fillings suggested sound like your perfect rugelach, get creative! Just about anything can work.

Prep Time: 20 minutes Cook Time: 16–20 minutes Makes: 2 dozen cookies

⅓ cup ghee + 1 tablespoon (90 g), or palm shortening

⅓ cup (80 ml) coconut cream, from a refrigerated can of coconut milk

1 tablespoon (17 g) kosher gelatin

3 tablespoons + 1 tablespoon (60 g) coconut sugar

1 teaspoon vanilla

⅛ teaspoon salt

1 cup (95 g) almond flour

¾ cup (98 g) arrowroot starch, plus more for dusting

1 tablespoon (7 g) coconut flour

FOR CHOCOLATE FILLING

4 ounces (113 g) dark chocolate, finely chopped

½ teaspoon cinnamon

¼ teaspoon sea salt

FOR RAISIN-NUT FILLING

½ cup (58 g) finely chopped walnuts

½ cup (75 g) raisins

1 tablespoon (15 g) coconut sugar

½ teaspoon cinnamon

⅛ teaspoon salt

In the bowl of a mixer, beat the ghee, coconut cream and gelatin on high until light and fluffy.

Add the coconut sugar, vanilla and salt and beat for a few minutes more, until well incorporated.

Add the almond flour, arrowroot and coconut flour one at a time, and beat on low until well incorporated.

Turn out onto a sheet of plastic wrap and form into a disc. Wrap up and refrigerate for at least 1 hour, or overnight.

After the dough has chilled, preheat the oven to 350°F (177°C) and remove the dough from the refrigerator. Turn it out onto a floured (arrowroot) surface and cut in half. Roll each portion into a circle about ½-inch (13-mm) thick, approximately 9 inches (23 cm) in diameter.

To make the filling, combine the ingredients of your preferred filling in a small bowl.

Sprinkle the dough with half of your desired filling, pressing lightly into the dough.

Cut the dough into quarters, and each quarter into thirds to get twelve triangles. Roll each one up, starting from the outside, using a paring knife or offset spatula to help if the dough wants to fall apart. It's delicate, but you can pinch it together as you go if it doesn't roll easily.

Transfer each cookie to a parchment-lined baking sheet. Place in the freezer for 10 minutes.

Remove and brush with ghee and sprinkle with coconut sugar.

Bake for 15 minutes or until just starting to get brown on the edges.

Bubbe's tip: Don't skip the freezer step! It's there for a reason—trust me, would you?

Chocolate Crunch Gelt

When Hanukkah rolls around, having homemade gelt, or chocolate "money,"
makes the memories that much more fun! And this way you can avoid the refined sugar, dairy
and other unnecessary additives. You'll need a gelt mold for this!

Prep Time: 5 minutes Cook Time: 20 minutes Makes: 4 servings

1 cup (180 g) chocolate chips
1 tablespoon (15 ml) coconut oil
½ teaspoon 100% vanilla extract
1 teaspoon (or more) coconut palm sugar

In a double boiler, over barely simmering water, melt the chocolate and coconut oil. Alternatively, you may melt in the microwave for 30-second intervals, stirring in between heating sessions until melted.

Next, stir in the vanilla and coconut palm sugar and spoon the mixture into the gelt molds.

Place the filled mold into the freezer for about 10–15 minutes or until the coins have solidified and set. Remove the tray from the freezer and pop out the chocolate coins. Refill the tray with any remaining melted chocolate mixture and repeat the steps above.

Mexican Chocolate Gelt

This Mexican Chocolate Gelt is just as delicious as its crunch counterpart, but instead adds in cinnamon
and a pinch of cayenne pepper for a kick that pairs deliciously with the creamy chocolate.

Prep Time: 5 minutes Cook Time: 20 minutes Makes: 4 servings

1 cup (180 g) chocolate chips
1 tablespoon (15 ml) coconut oil
½ teaspoon 100% vanilla extract
½ teaspoon (or more) ground cinnamon
¼ teaspoon cayenne pepper

Follow instructions for the Chocolate Crunch Gelt above, adding in the ground cinnamon and cayenne pepper in place of the coconut palm sugar. Spoon the mixture into the mold as indicated above and follow remaining instructions.

Bubbe's tip: What, you can't take a little heat? You can omit the cayenne and keep the cinnamon. Maybe even add in a pinch of allspice. So, what are you kvetchin' about?!

Chocolate–Covered Matzo

If you've never had chocolate-covered matzo before, rank this recipe first on your to-do list. It's a must.

Prep Time: 15 minutes **Freeze Time:** 20 minutes **Makes:** 4 servings

4 sheets homemade Matzo (from page 44 or 47)

1 cup (180 g) chocolate chips, melted

Unsweetened coconut flakes, crushed nuts or seeds, optional

Line a baking sheet with parchment paper. Then, using a basting brush, take one sheet of matzo at a time and "paint" on the chocolate.

If you wish to add toppings, you can then sprinkle nuts, seeds or coconut shreds. Place the chocolate covered matzo onto the parchment-lined baking sheet and repeat with remaining pieces of matzo.

Place the baking sheet into the freezer for 20 minutes or until the chocolate hardens. Now you can remove it and break it into smaller pieces, if you wish, or serve and eat as is!

Bubbe's tip: What, you don't like simple?! Then add crushed nuts, seeds or coconut and mix and match! What are you waiting for? Get on with it!

Apple Kugel

For Rosh Hashanah, we often make delicious foods with apples and honey for a "sweet new year." This Apple Kugel recipe takes away the refined white flour for a delicious, cake-like treat that won't weigh so heavily once eaten!

Prep Time: 15 minutes Cook Time: 40 minutes Makes: 8 servings

5 eggs

3 tablespoons (45 ml) avocado oil, or preferred cooking fat

½ cup (120 ml) honey

¼ cup (28 g) coconut flour

½ cup (64 g) arrowroot powder

1 teaspoon baking soda

½ teaspoon ground cinnamon

¼ teaspoon ground nutmeg

Pinch sea salt

2 apples, sliced thin

Preheat the oven to 350°F (177°C) and grease an 8 x 8 inch (20 x 20 cm) casserole dish. Next, beat eggs, avocado oil and honey in a mixing bowl until well combined.

In another mixing bowl, combine coconut flour, arrowroot powder, baking soda, cinnamon, nutmeg and sea salt.

Add the wet ingredients into the dry ingredients and whisk until well incorporated. Pour the kugel batter into the prepared baking dish.

Next, arrange your apple slices into the batter. You may arrange them any way you please, as long as the bottom later becomes submerged. The remaining layers may drift up toward the surface more, which makes for a nice presentation after baking.

Put your casserole dish into the oven and bake for 30–40 minutes or until just set in the center.

Bubbe's tip: What, you're looking to impress your Rosh Hasanah guests? Use half apple and half pears for a fancy kugel. Do I have to think of everything?

Blintzes with Blueberry Topping

Blintzes have long been a favorite Jewish comfort food. Traditionally made with white flour and refined sugar and filled with dairy, they can often create issues for those with food intolerances. This version is so incredibly delicious you'll never miss the original!

Prep Time: 20 minutes + soaking time for the cashews Cook Time: 35 minutes Makes: 9 blintzes, about 4 servings

FOR THE BLINTZES

5 eggs

1 cup (240 ml) dairy-free milk (coconut, almond, cashew or flax)

1 cup (120 g) cassava flour, not tapioca starch (can be found online or in international markets)

Pinch sea salt

1 tablespoon (15 ml) avocado or olive oil

FOR THE FILLING

1 cup (143 g) raw cashews, soaked for at least 4 hours and drained

¼ cup (60 ml) canned coconut milk

3 tablespoons (45 ml) honey

1 teaspoon lemon juice

FOR THE TOPPING

10 ounces (285 g) fresh or frozen blueberries

¼ cup (60 ml) maple syrup

Zest from 1 lemon

To begin, mix all the blintz ingredients in a blender and blend until smooth. In a large, oiled skillet heated over medium-high heat, pour about a ninth of the mixture into the skillet. Swirl the batter around in the pan until it resembles a large, thin, flat pancake.

After a minute or two, using a thin flexible spatula, flip over the blintz carefully. Remove from heat after a minute or two once both sides are cooked. Repeat with remaining batter.

To make the filling, puree the cashews, coconut milk, honey and lemon juice until smooth and creamy.

To make the topping, place the blueberries, maple syrup and lemon zest in a small skillet or saucepan and heat over high heat for about 10 minutes, mashing the berries and stirring regularly. The sauce will thicken and the fruit will soften.

To assemble your blintzes, take one of the crepes, fill it with a tablespoon (15 ml) of the filling and fold it like a burrito so all sides are sealed.

In a medium, lightly oiled skillet, pan-fry the blintz until it is nicely browned on both sides. Using a flexible spatula will help in flipping it, as it can be fragile. Remove from the skillet and set aside.

Repeat with remaining blintzes, top with warm blueberry sauce and enjoy!

Bubbe's tip: Not a blueberry fan?! Don't get all meshuga over it! Just substitute your favorite fruit and follow the above instructions!

Halvah

Halvah is a traditional sesame candy made with lots of refined white sugar.
We made this version with honey and coconut palm sugar for a naturally sweetened treat!

Prep Time: 5 minutes Cook Time: 10 minutes + overnight refrigeration Makes: 20 servings

½ cup (120 ml) honey
½ cup (120 g) coconut palm sugar
½ cup (120 ml) water
1 cup (240 g) tahini
1 teaspoon 100% vanilla extract

To start, you will need a candy thermometer so that you can confirm the temperature. Then, in a small saucepan, heat the honey, palm sugar and water until it reaches between 260°F–265°F (127°C–129°C).

In another saucepan on a separate burner, heat the tahini over low heat with the vanilla extract, stirring occasionally. Be careful as tahini can burn if heated too high.

Once the honey mixture successfully reaches 260°F (127°C) or so, fold in the tahini and remove from the heat. Stir the combined halvah mixture vigorously until well combined and pour into a small- or mini-sized, parchment-lined loaf pan.

Chill in the refrigerator, or covered at room temperature, overnight, then slice and serve. It will be similar to a hard candy or toffee in texture, so take care in slicing. Thinner slices will yield flakier ones.

Bubbe's tip: In case you need a reminder, this is a treat! Make sure not to treat it like one of the major food groups! Just a bisl will do the trick!

Honey Cake

Honey Cake is practically a requirement for Rosh Hashanah, which is the Jewish New Year, and is celebrated in the fall. The idea is to ring in the year to come with sweet foods, symbolizing a sweet new year. This cake is so good as a dessert, or with tea, that you might find yourself wanting to ring in each week with it!

Prep Time: 10 minutes **Cook Time:** 45–55 minutes **Makes:** 1 (12-inch [30-cm]) Bundt cake

FOR THE CAKE

Oil or palm shortening, for greasing the pan

4 eggs

1 cup (240 g) coconut sugar

1 cup (240 ml) honey

1½ teaspoons (7 ml) vanilla

1 cup (240 ml) strong black tea, cooled

3 tablespoons (45 ml) bourbon or whiskey (optional, add additional tea if omitting)

3 cups (288 g) almond flour

1½ cups (192 g) arrowroot powder (plus more for flouring pan)

¾ cup (85 g) coconut flour

1½ teaspoons (6.5 g) baking soda

2 teaspoons (5 g) ground cinnamon

¾ teaspoon ground allspice

¾ teaspoon ground cardamom

1½ teaspoons (7 g) salt

FOR THE ICING

¼ cup (55 g) coconut butter

2 tablespoons (30 ml) honey

⅓ cup (80 ml) full-fat coconut milk

¼ teaspoon cinnamon

¼ teaspoon cardamom

½ teaspoon vanilla extract

Preheat the oven to 350°F (177°C). Grease and flour a 12-cup (2.8-L) Bundt pan.

In a large bowl, beat the eggs, coconut sugar, honey, vanilla, tea and bourbon until well incorporated.

In a medium bowl, whisk together the almond flour, arrowroot, coconut flour, baking soda, cinnamon, allspice, cardamom and salt. Add to the liquid mixture and beat for another minute.

Pour the batter into your prepared pan and bake for 40–50 minutes, or until the top bounces back when you gently push it, and a knife inserted into the center comes out clean.

Allow the cakes to cool on a wire rack before inverting onto a plate.

To make the icing, melt the coconut butter in a small saucepan and then add the honey, coconut milk, cinnamon, cardamom and vanilla. Remove from heat and whisk to combine.

Transfer to a sealable plastic bag, trying to get it into one corner as much as possible. Cut just the tip of the corner off and drizzle the icing over the cake.

Bubbe's tip: Don't make a mess! Slide some parchment or wax paper under the outside of the cake before you ice it. Once the icing starts to harden, you can pull them out, and you will be left with a clean serving platter. Otherwise, the yentas will never let you hear the end of it!

Chocolate Babka

This is the stuff that you have dreamt about since abstaining from grain, right?!
That pull-apart bread with the chocolate swirl that must be made of sunshine and rainbows.
This recipe uses a special blend of ingredients to re-create a universal favorite!

Prep Time: 20 minutes Cook Time: 45 minutes Makes: 8 servings

FOR THE LOAF

1 cup (240 ml) warm water (around 110°F [43°C])

2 teaspoons (5 g) active yeast

3 tablespoons (45 ml) maple syrup

Pinch sea salt

1 cup (95 g) almond flour

¾ cup (92 g) cassava flour

1 teaspoon baking soda

5 tablespoons (75 g) psyllium husk

¼ cup (60 g) coconut palm sugar

3 egg whites

2 tablespoons (30 ml) apple cider vinegar

FOR THE FILLING

1 cup (180 g) chocolate chips

¼ cup (60 ml) dairy-free milk (almond, flax or coconut)

Combine the warm water, yeast and maple syrup in a small mixing bowl. Stir gently and allow to sit for around 5 minutes or until the yeast activates. You will know it is working correctly when it bubbles or gets frothy.

While your yeast mixture activates, combine your sea salt, almond flour, cassava flour, baking soda, psyllium husk and coconut palm sugar in a separate mixing bowl. Use a spoon or fork to mix your dry ingredients.

Add the egg whites and apple cider vinegar to the wet mixture. Whisk quickly and then pour the wet ingredients into the dry ingredients. Stir to quickly combine as the psyllium husk will start to "gel" slightly.

Once all ingredients are incorporated, you may use your hands to create one large ball of dough. Remove it from the mixing bowl and set it on a piece of parchment paper. Take a second piece of parchment paper to place on top of the dough and roll it out into a large rectangle about ½-inch (13-mm) thick.

Let the dough rest while you melt your chocolate chips and dairy-free milk. You can do this over a double broiler or in a saucepan over low heat. Once the chocolate is melted and incorporated well with the milk, you can brush it over the rolled-out dough, making sure to distribute evenly.

Next, start with the long side and roll it up like a jellyroll. Once you have a long "snake," bring together the two ends and then twist it into a loaf. If the dough cracks, carefully pinch it back together.

Place the loaf into a parchment-lined bread pan and make slits in the dough across the top before baking. Bake it for around 45 minutes, or until cooked through. Remove from the oven and allow to cool slightly before slicing. This can be toasted and buttered, if desired.

Bubbe's tip: Go nuts! No, not meshuga nuts … but almonds, pecans and cashews! Toss a few chopped nuts into your chocolate swirl and maybe even a little ground cinnamon!

Apple Ring Fritters

These are like Jewish carnival food if there ever was such a thing! Fried apples in a delicious crispy batter—perfect for Hanukkah or for days ending in "y."

Prep Time: 10 minutes Cook Time: 15 minutes Makes: 4 servings

Avocado oil, coconut oil or palm shortening for frying
2 Granny Smith apples
2 eggs
2 tablespoons (30 ml) maple syrup
½ teaspoon ground cinnamon
½ teaspoon 100% vanilla extract
¾ cup (95 g) tapioca starch
½ cup (48 g) almond flour
½ cup (120 ml) water

FOR SERVING
Additional tapioca starch
Coconut palm sugar, to taste
Additional ground cinnamon

Heat your cooking fat in a small saucepan over medium-high heat. Make sure the oil is about an inch (2.5-cm) deep in the saucepan. By using a smaller pan, you can thereby use less oil.

Core and slice your apples into rings. This can be done one of two ways: either use an apple corer first and then slice rings afterwards, or you can use a mandolin and slice the apples into rings and then remove the seeds afterwards.

To make the batter, whisk the eggs, maple syrup, cinnamon, vanilla extract, tapioca starch, almond flour and water. Dip each apple ring into the batter and then carefully and quickly transfer over to the hot oil. Fry for about 2–3 minutes on each side and then place on a towel-lined plate.

Repeat until all the apple rings are fried. Before serving, sprinkle tapioca starch (cosmetic), a bit of coconut sugar or some ground cinnamon.

Bubbe's tip: How hot is your oil? You'll want it to be "shimmering" before you try to fry or you will end up with soggy fritters. Not appealing!

Raspberry Chocolate Macaroons

Raspberry jam and fresh raspberries put a new twist on this favorite cookie.
And since the jam is sweet, you don't need to add any additional sweetener!

Prep Time: 10 minutes **Cook Time:** 20–25 minutes **Makes:** About 18 cookies

1 (14-ounce [414-ml]) can full-fat coconut milk

¼ cup (60 ml) raspberry jam

½ cup (60 g) raspberries

2 egg whites

⅛ teaspoon salt

7 ounces (200 g), or about 2¾ cups, unsweetened coconut

FOR CHOCOLATE DRIZZLE

3 ounces (85 g) unsweetened chocolate, chopped

3 tablespoons (45 ml) honey

Preheat the oven to 350°F (177°C) and line two baking sheets with parchment paper.

In a medium saucepan, bring the coconut milk, raspberry jam and raspberries to a simmer over medium heat. Allow them to simmer for about 5 minutes, stirring occasionally.

In a medium bowl, beat the egg whites and the salt until medium peaks form.

Place the coconut in a large bowl, and strain the coconut milk mixture into it. Stir to combine. Gently fold in the egg whites.

Using an ice cream scoop with a lever or two spoons, drop the batter onto the cookie sheets, about 2 tablespoons (30 ml) each.

Bake for 20 minutes, or until golden brown. Allow them to cool on the pans placed over wire racks. They will firm up more when cool.

Melt about two-thirds of the chocolate in a double boiler and remove from the heat. Stir in the remaining chocolate until it's melted. Stir in the honey and set aside.

Once the macaroons are cool, drizzle with chocolate and refrigerate.

Bubbe's tip: Don't waste those yolks! Save them to make Mayonnaise (page 228).

Creamsicle Macaroons

Macaroons that taste like creamsicles? What could be bad?!

Prep Time: 10 minutes **Cook Time:** 25–30 minutes **Makes:** 18 cookies

2 egg whites

12 ounces (340 g) unsweetened shredded coconut

1 (14-ounce [414-ml]) can full-fat coconut milk

¼ cup (60 ml) honey

Zest of one orange (about ½ tablespoon [7 ml])

1 tablespoon (15 ml) orange juice

2 teaspoons (10 ml) vanilla extract

Pinch salt

Preheat the oven to 350°F (177°C). Line two baking sheets with parchment paper.

In a medium bowl, beat the egg whites until medium peaks form.

In a large bowl, combine the shredded coconut, coconut milk, honey, orange zest, orange juice, vanilla and salt.

Fold the egg whites into the coconut mixture.

Using a small ice cream scoop with a lever, or two spoons, drop the mixture onto a cookie sheet, about 2 tablespoons (30 ml) in each.

Bake for 25–30 minutes, or until golden brown on the edges. Allow them to cool before removing from the pan.

Bubbe's tip: Don't waste those yolks! Save them to make Mayonnaise (page 228).

Jelly Donuts

If latkes are the staple side dish of Hanukkah, Jelly Donuts—or sufganiyot—are the classic dessert.

Prep Time: 5 minutes Cook Time: 15 minutes Makes: 25–30 donut holes

4 eggs

¼ cup (60 ml) honey

¼ cup (60 ml) full-fat canned coconut milk

½ cup (65 g) arrowroot powder

½ cup (55 g) coconut flour, more if needed (see note)

½ teaspoon baking soda

¼ teaspoon salt

2 tablespoons (30 ml) strawberry or cherry jelly, or your favorite flavor

2 tablespoons (30 g) coconut sugar, ground to a fine powder in a spice or coffee grinder

In a large saucepan, heat the oil to 360°F (182°C). Prepare a rimmed baking sheet with a rack for transferring the donuts to after frying.

In a medium bowl, whisk together the eggs, honey and coconut milk. To it, add the arrowroot powder, coconut flour, baking soda and salt. Mix well to combine.

Allow the batter to rest for 1–2 minutes. It will thicken up a bit (see note).

Once the oil is hot, use a small ice cream scoop with a lever to drop the donuts into the oil, about 6–8 at a time. Each one should be a bit less than a tablespoon (15 ml) worth of batter; they will expand in the oil.

Fry for 3–4 minutes each, rolling them halfway through with a long-handled, metal, slotted spoon. Once cooked through, remove to the prepared baking sheet. Repeat with the remaining batter.

Using a skewer, poke a hole into one side of a donut and wiggle it around a bit to widen the hole. Using a ⅛-teaspoon measuring spoon, spoon some jelly into the hole. Repeat with the remaining donuts.

Dust with powdered coconut sugar before serving.

Note: Coconut flours vary greatly, and some are more absorbant than others. If after 2 minutes the batter is still too thin to scoop, stir in another tablespoon (15 g) and allow it to sit for a minute more.

Bubbe's tip: Oy gevalt, filling the donuts can be a lot of trouble. If it's too much for you, just dip them in the jelly, or eat them plain. They'll still be delicious!

Chocolate Donuts

Jelly donuts might be the classic Hanukkah dessert, but there's no reason to leave chocolate out of the party. And if you can't decide between the two, we won't fault you for filling your chocolate donuts with cherry jelly, either.

Prep Time: 10 minutes **Cook Time:** 15 minutes **Makes:** 25–30 donut holes

1½–2 cups (350–475 ml) light olive or avocado oil, for frying

4 eggs

¼ cup (60 ml) honey

½ cup (120 ml) full-fat coconut milk

⅔ cup (85 g) arrowroot powder

½ cup (55 g) coconut flour, more if needed (see note)

½ teaspoon baking soda

¼ cup + 1 tablespoon (35 g) cocoa powder

¼ teaspoon salt

FOR THE CHOCOLATE GLAZE

4 ounces (113 g) unsweetened chocolate

2 tablespoons (30 ml) coconut oil

¼ cup (60 ml) honey

In a large saucepan, heat the oil to 360°F (182°C). Prepare a rimmed baking sheet with a rack for transferring the donuts to after frying.

In a medium bowl, whisk together the eggs, honey and coconut milk. To it, add the arrowroot powder, coconut flour, baking soda, cocoa powder and salt. Mix well to combine.

Allow the batter to rest for 1–2 minutes. It will thicken up a bit (see note).

Once the oil is hot, use a small ice cream scoop with a lever to drop the donuts into the oil, about 6–8 at a time. Each one should be a bit less than a tablespoon (15 ml) worth of batter; they will expand in the oil.

Fry for 3–4 minutes each, rolling them halfway through with a long-handled metal, slotted spoon. Once cooked through, remove to the prepared baking sheet. Repeat with the remaining batter.

To make the glaze, combine the chocolate and coconut oil in the bowl of a double boiler over simmering water. Once melted, add the honey and stir to combine. Allow the chocolate to cool for 5–10 minutes before rolling the donuts in the glaze and placing them back on a parchment-lined baking sheet. Refrigerate until the glaze hardens, about 15 minutes.

Note: Coconut flours vary greatly, and some are more absorbant than others. If after 2 minutes the batter is still too thin to scoop, stir in another tablespoon (15 g) and allow it to sit for a minute more.

Bubbe's tip: Bubula, if you want to make these even more fancy schmancy, do like the kids do these days and spinkle them with coarse sea salt.

Flourless Chocolate Cake

Your Paleo Passover never tasted so good! But don't stop there—
this flourless cake is the perfect treat to nosh year round.

Prep Time: 20 minutes Cook Time: 35–40 minutes Makes: 8 servings

8 eggs, separated

¾ cups (180 g) coconut palm sugar or maple sugar, divided

½ cup (55 g) organic cocoa powder

½ cup (120 ml) coconut oil, melted

Tapioca starch for garnishing, optional

Preheat the oven to 325°F (163°C). Grease a spring-form pan with coconut oil.

Then, beat the egg whites, either in a stand mixer or with a handheld mixer, until light and foamy and then sprinkle in ¼ cup (60 g) sugar while continuing to beat.

In another bowl whisk together the cocoa powder and melted coconut oil. Make sure there are no lumps and then whisk in egg yolks and the remaining ½ cup (120 g) sugar. Next, gradually add the chocolate mixture into the egg white mixture and continue mixing on medium-high until creamy.

Pour into the prepared pan and bake for 35–40 minutes, or until the center is baked through. Remove carefully from the oven and allow the cake to cool slightly before removing the outer ring of the pan.

If you'd like to garnish with a "powdered sugar" feel, sift a little tapioca starch on top. This is cosmetic only but creates a more traditional appearance.

Bubbe's tip: White powdered sugar is dreck! But if you want your tapioca to be slightly sweet, you can always sprinkle in some coconut palm sugar or even stevia! Not that you aren't sweet enough!

Black and White Cookies

Eating a Black and White Cookie is a rite of passage and earns you a star on the sidewalk out front of Deliville. If you've been missing the original, this one will make your heart sing!

Prep Time: 10 minutes   Cook Time: 15 minutes   Makes: Up to 6 cookies

FOR THE COOKIES
2 cups (192 g) almond flour
3 eggs
1 teaspoon 100% vanilla extract
½ cup (72 g) maple sugar
¼ cup (30 g) tapioca starch
1 teaspoon baking soda
Pinch salt

FOR THE BLACK ICING
⅓ cup (80 g) chocolate chips

FOR THE WHITE ICING
⅓ cup (80 ml) coconut oil, melted
1 teaspoon coconut cream
1 teaspoon light-colored honey
¼ teaspoon 100% vanilla extract

Preheat the oven to 350°F (177°C) and line a baking sheet with parchment paper. Combine the almond flour, eggs, vanilla, maple sugar, tapioca starch, baking soda and salt.

Divide the dough into 6 portions and on the prepared baking sheet flatten each one into a disc about ¼ inch (6 mm) think.

Press the ball until it flattens into a thinner disc, around ¼ inch (6 mm) thick. These have a cake-like texture, so if you prefer thinner, you can flatten them more, but the texture may change. Bake the cookies for 10–12 minutes, watching so they do not burn. While the cookies are baking, make your two icings.

To make the chocolate icing, melt the chocolate chips, which can be done with a double boiler method. To do this, bring 2 cups (450 ml) of water to a boil over high heat in a small saucepan. Place your chocolate chips in a stainless steel mixing bowl and situate it over the boiling water. Stir the chocolate until it is melted and remove from heat.

To make the vanilla icing, you can use the same method to melt the coconut oil and then add in the remaining vanilla icing ingredients.

Set aside and allow it to cool until it thickens and begins to turn opaque again. Once the cookies have cooled entirely, spread your two icings evenly, each covering half a cookie.

Bubbe's tip: These cookies are soft, but if baked too long, they will start to crisp up. Also, be sure you let them cool entirely before icing them, or your icing will melt and slide right off! Don't be all meshuga, and listen to your bubbe!

Chocolate Chip Mandelbrot

It's unclear which came first, the biscotti or the Mandelbrot, but the two sure do have a lot in common. Both are baked twice and super crispy. Mandelbrot (formed from the words mandel meaning "almond" and brot meaning "bread") gets extra crunch from the roasted almonds that fill them.

Prep Time: 20 minutes   Cook Time: 40 minutes, plus time to cool   Makes: 1 dozen cookies

1½ cups (145 g) almond flour

½ teaspoon baking soda

¼ teaspoon sea salt

2 tablespoons (30 g) coconut sugar

3 tablespoons (42 g) palm shortening

2 tablespoons (30 ml) honey

½ cup (70 g) dry roasted, salted almonds

¼ cup (45 g) chocolate chips

Preheat the oven to 350°F (177°C) and line a baking sheet with parchment paper.

In the bowl of a food processor, blend together the almond flour, baking soda, salt and coconut sugar.

Add the shortening and honey and blend again until it is well incorporated.

Add the almonds and pulse 5–6 times to get them roughly chopped and incorporated into the dough. Add the chips and pulse two quick times to mix them in.

Turn the dough out onto the prepared baking sheet and mold into a log, about 8 x 2 inches (20 x 5 cm), leaving the dough with a thickness of 1 inch (2.5 cm).

Bake the dough for 15 minutes and then allow it to cool for at least 45 minutes. Once the loaf is cool, turn the oven to 275°F (135°C) and slice the loaf into 10–12 slices, about ¾- to 1-inch (1.9- to 2.5-cm) thick. Spread the slices out on the baking sheet and bake for 25 minutes.

Allow to cool before serving.

Bubbe's tip: So what, almonds give you hives?! How about you try pistachios instead? You can even experiment with different nut flours by grinding your favorites in a high-speed blender or food processor.

Dairy-Free Condiments and Sauces

What's a latke without applesauce? Or a bagel without a schmear? What's a Reuben without the Russian Dressing (page 232)? Drek! That's what! Homemade condiments are essential to any Yiddish kitchen. They give life and personality to traditional Jewish foods. This chapter helps you navigate a lifestyle free of grain and dairy by reviving recipes for Cashew Cream Cheese (page 231), Dairy-Free Sour Cream (page 216) and even homemade Horseradish Sour Cream (page 224), all while maintaining the integrity of these traditional basics. What're you waiting for, Elijah? It's time for schmaltz!

Applesauce

Once you realize how simple it is to make homemade applesauce, you may never buy the jarred stuff again! You can use any apple variety for this recipe, but note that a combination of apples yields the most flavorful end product!

Prep Time: 10 minutes   Cook Time: 40–50 minutes   Makes: 1 quart (950 ml)

2 pounds (900 g) apples (about 8 medium Braeburn, Cortland, McIntosh or Gravenstein)

1 cinnamon stick, optional

¼ cup (60 ml) water, if needed

Peel and dice your apples and place in a medium saucepan. Add the cinnamon stick, if using.

Slowly cook, covered, over a low flame for 40–50 minutes, or until the apples are cooked. Check and stir occasionally.

The apples should release their own liquid and basically cook themselves. If at any point there's any sticking to the bottom of the pan, add the water.

If you prefer a smooth applesauce, puree in a blender, food processor or with an immersion blender.

Chill before serving.

Bubbe's tip: Got more fruit than you can eat? Don't waste it! Add it to the applesauce! Strawberries, peaches, cherries and raspberries are all delicious additions.

Dairy-Free Sour Cream

This sour cream is free of casein and lactose, but is creamy and cultured like traditional sour cream. You'll find it perfect for topping latkes or even placing a dollop on your favorite soups, like Borscht (page 37)!

Prep Time: 10 minutes Cook Time: 8 hours Makes: 10 servings

1 cup (110 g) raw cashews, soaked for 4 hours and drained

½ cup (120 ml) fresh, cool water

½ teaspoon probiotic powder

1 teaspoon, or more, apple cider vinegar

Preheat your oven on the lowest setting and then turn your oven light on. Once your oven reaches the desired temperature, turn it off, but keep the light on. Then, blend all the ingredients until completely smooth. If you need to add more water, do so 1 tablespoon (15 ml) at a time without making it too watery. It should have the texture of dairy sour cream. Once your desired consistency is reached, transfer the contents to a small mason jar or other glass jar with a lid.

Screw the lid on and place it in the oven to rest overnight, about 8 hours; this will help the good bacteria grow. In the morning, remove it from the oven and transfer to the refrigerator until ready for use.

Alternatively, you can use a 7-in-1 Instant Pot with the yogurt setting to make this. After blending the ingredients, transfer the mixture to a glass jar.

Pour 1 cup (240 ml) of water into the bottom of your Instant Pot and then set the stainless "basket" insert into the bottom.

Place your glass jar on top of the grate and close the lid. Press the "yogurt" button and select how many hours you'd like it to culture, 6–8 being preferable. After the time has passed, remove the jar, secure a lid on top and place it in the refrigerator until ready to use.

Bubbe's tip: Like your sour cream extra sour? Increase the probiotics and apple cider vinegar by a bisl for extra tart!

Charoset

Charoset is traditionally served during a Passover Seder, but, in all honesty, it's a great chilled, fruit-based salad that is a perfect accompaniment for any meal!

Prep Time: 15 minutes **Cook Time:** None **Makes:** 4–6 servings

3 large Honey Crisp apples, or preferred apple variety

1 cup (125 g) walnut pieces

4 tablespoons (60 ml) 100% grape juice or sweet red wine

Juice from ½ lemon

½ teaspoon ground cinnamon, or more if desired

1 tablespoon (15 g) coconut palm sugar

Mince apples and place in a large mixing bowl. Mix in the remaining ingredients and stir to combine.

Bubbe's tip: Any good charoset deserves a delicious matzo delivery. Be sure to make bubbe proud by making your own (page 44 or 47).

Fresh Horseradish Sauce

Making your own horseradish will make chopping onions seem like a vacation. Prepare to shed a few tears! It's well worth it, though; you won't get anything nearly this fresh out of a jar!

Prep Time: 10 minutes Cook Time: None Makes: 1 cup (240 ml)

½ pound (230 g) horseradish root, peeled and diced

¼ cup (60 ml) white vinegar

⅛ teaspoon salt

Water, as needed

Place the horseradish in the bowl of your food processor with the chopping blade. Pulse several times to get it uniformly minced.

Process the horseradish for about 5 minutes, adding the vinegar and the salt after a minute or so. Scrape down the sides with a rubber spatula several times.

If the mixture is too dry, add a little bit of water to loosen it up a bit.

Transfer to a serving or storage dish and keep chilled until ready to serve.

Bubbe's tip: Bubula, this is not the time to do your silly deep breathing exercises you learned in that yoga you do! Horseradish fumes are very strong, and if you're not as strong as an ox, like I am, oy gevalt, will you be crying.

Fresh Horseradish Beet Sauce

This version of homemade horseradish sauce combines the earthy undertone and the beautiful vibrant color of beets with the kick of the horseradish root. You might just discover this is your new favorite condiment!

Prep Time: 10 minutes **Cook Time:** None **Makes:** 1 cup (240 ml)

½ pound (230 g) fresh horseradish root, peeled and diced

1 small beet, diced

¼ cup (60 ml) white wine vinegar

⅛ teaspoon sea salt

Water, as needed

Place the horseradish and beet in the bowl of your food processor with the chopping blade. Pulse several times to get it uniformly minced.

Process the horseradish and beet for about 5 minutes, adding the vinegar and the salt after a minute or so. Scrape down the sides with a rubber spatula several times.

If the mixture is too dry, add a little bit of water to loosen it up a bit.

Transfer to a serving or storage dish and keep chilled until ready to serve.

Bubbe's tip: Beet juice stains, bubula! Make sure you don't get any on your nice clothes that you paid too much for.

Horseradish Sour Cream

In this recipe, the zest of the horseradish is balanced by the cool, creaminess of the dairy-free sour cream. You can even place a dollop of this on your latkes for a zippy alternative to the more traditional sour cream topping.

Prep Time: 1 minute **Cook Time:** None **Makes:** About ½ cup (120 ml)

½ cup (120 g) sour cream or Dairy-Free Sour Cream (page 216)

1 tablespoon (15 ml) Fresh Horseradish Sauce (page 220)

Combine sour cream and horseradish and stir to combine.

Bubbe's tip: This sauce is a real workhorse! Dollop it on your latkes, mix it into tuna salad for a zingy lunch or put it on your roast beef sandwich.

Dairy-Free Butter

Does dairy get you feeling all verkakte? Sadly, many butter alternatives are still made with subpar ingredients. This Dairy-Free Butter recipe can be used whenever a recipe calls for butter and is still creamy and delicious!

Prep Time: 5 minutes **Freeze Time:** 30 minutes–1 hour **Makes:** Approximately 8 servings

2 tablespoons (30 ml) full-fat coconut milk

3 tablespoons (45 ml) olive oil

2 tablespoons (30 ml) melted coconut oil

3 tablespoons (45 ml) avocado oil

½ teaspoon salt

Combine all ingredients in a blender and blend until creamy.

Then, pour into a glass dish with lid and freeze for 30 minutes to 1 hour (or refrigerate until solid). Finally, remove from the freezer and use as desired or store in fridge.

Bubbe's tip: You want a pat of butter instead? Stop stressing, oy gevalt! Pour this mixture into a mold of your choosing, and you've got your pats made easily!

Mayonnaise

If you're intimidated by the idea of making homemade mayonnaise, don't be! It's actually way easier than you might think and tastes about a hundred times better than the store-bought variety. An immersion blender is the key to foolproof mayo, but a regular blender will work too.

Prep Time: 5 minutes Cook Time: None Makes: About 1 cup (240 ml)

3 egg yolks
1 tablespoon (15 ml) apple cider vinegar
½ teaspoon finely ground sea salt
¾ cup (180 ml) oil (light olive oil, macadamia, avocado or a combination), divided
2 tablespoons (30 ml) water
1 tablespoon (15 ml) lemon juice

Place the egg yolks and vinegar in a wide-mouthed, quart-sized glass jar or similarly sized vessel. If using a regular blender, place the egg yolks in the jar of your blender.

Blend with an immersion blender for 1 minute. Then add the salt and blend again.

With the motor running, slowly drizzle in ½ cup (120 ml) of the oil, keeping the stream small. Incorporate the oil by moving the blender in small up and down circles.

Add the water and blend until combined.

Slowly drizzle in the remaining ¼ cup (60 ml) of oil, continuing to run the blender.

Blend in the lemon juice.

Store in a jar in the fridge for up to 5 days.

Bubbe's tip: In my day, we just plucked the eggs from the backyard and didn't have to worry about it! Since you're probably getting your eggs from the supermarket, make sure you're buying the best quality ones you can.

Cashew Cream Cheese

While there may not be a substitute for real cream cheese, this comes pretty close. Culturing the puree gives it the cheesy tang that we all know and love. A good schmear on some seeded crackers (page 43) with lox and chives has all the flavors of the bagel shop favorite, with added crunch.

Prep Time: 5 minutes, plus 12–18 hours to culture Cook Time: None Makes: about 1¼ cups (300 ml)

2 cups (220 g) raw cashews, soaked in 4 cups (950 ml) cold water for at least 8–12 hours

20 billion organisms probiotics, about ½ teaspoon

1 tablespoon (15 ml) water

1 tablespoon (15 ml) lemon juice

½ teaspoon salt

¼ teaspoon cream of tartar

After the cashews have soaked for at least 8 hours, drain them and place in a food processor or high-speed blender. Blend until smooth, scraping down the sides a few times. If you need to add a bit of water to get it smooth, do so, but try to add as little as possible.

Dissolve the probiotics in 1 tablespoon (15 ml) warm (not hot) water and mix into the cashew mixture.

Line a fine mesh strainer with cheesecloth and scrape the cashew mixture into it. Wrap the cheesecloth around it and cover with a clean kitchen towel.

Allow to culture at room temperature for at least 12, and up to 18, hours. It will get more tart the longer you leave it. Once it is cultured to your liking, transfer to a bowl and stir in the lemon juice, salt and cream of tartar. Store refrigerated in a glass jar for up to one week.

Bubbe's tip: I know how you love those fancy cream cheeses from the bagel shop, bubula. Make them at home! Just add chives, veggies or garlic and herbs when you mix in the lemon juice.

Russian Dressing

It's the perfect condiment with a "bisl of this and a bisl of that." While it's traditionally served on a Reuben (page 101), you might find about 8,509 other ways to take this condiment for a dip!

Prep Time: 5 minutes Cook Time: None Makes: 6 servings

⅓ cup (80 ml) Mayonnaise (page 228)

⅓ cup (80 ml) ketchup (see note)

3 teaspoons (15 ml) pickle relish

½ teaspoon Worcestershire sauce (see note)

1 teaspoon dried minced onion

Pinch sea salt

Pinch onion powder

Pinch garlic powder

Combine all ingredients in a small mixing bowl and stir to combine. Use as a dip, dressing or sandwich condiment for the Reuben on page 101.

Note: Make sure to check the labels of your ketchup and Worcestershire sauce. Some have undesireable ingredients such as corn syrup and soy.

Bubbe's tip: If you are new to making homemade mayonnaise, be sure to try the recipe on page 228. It will convince you and everyone around you that you are a mayo maven!

Schmaltz and Gribenes

Sure, you can use olive or avocado oil for cooking, but once you try cooking with schmaltz, you might not ever go back! It is a richly flavored, high-heat cooking fat that will bring your knishes to the next level, and then some! Gribenes are the delicious by-product of making schmaltz; once all of the fat is rendered, you're left with crispy salty bites that are best compared to bacon—not made of pork, of course! Save the skin and fat when you trim chicken for any chicken dish you prepare. You can save it in a bag in the freezer until you get about ¾ pound (340 g).

Prep Time: 10 minutes Cook Time: 1 hour Makes: ½ cup (120 ml) schmaltz and ½–¾ cup (60-80 ml) gribenes

¾ pound (340 g) chicken fat and skin
¼ cup (60 ml) water
1 teaspoon salt
½ medium onion, cut into small dices

Mince your chicken fat as small as possible. This is much easier done when the fat is frozen. The best way is to slice it and then pulse it in a food processor.

In a large skillet, combine the fat with the water and salt and set over medium heat. Allow it to cook for 15 minutes or so, until the fat begins to render and the skin and fat begin to brown a bit.

After 15 minutes, add the onion and turn the heat down to medium-low. Continue to cook for 45–60 minutes more, stirring occasionally, until the onions are deep brown in color. Adjust the heat as needed, so that the fat is sizzling but not browning too quickly. It should remain clear and yellow.

Strain the schmaltz with a fine mesh sieve and store the schmaltz and gribenes in the refrigerator in seperate jars.

Bubbe's tip: I wouldn't know what bacon tastes like because I don't eat treif, but your uncle Morty says the gribenes taste just like bacon. Kosher bacon! Can you believe it?!

Holiday Menus and Tips

In this chapter, you'll find everything you need to know to be a good Jew. I'm kidding, already! But if you want to brush up on your holiday facts while you're preparing your holiday meals, this is the place to do it. You don't want to get caught cooking on Shabbat or Yom Kippur now do you?!

Purim

Purim Menu

Everything Crackers (page 43)

Chopped Liver (page 20)

Challah (page 52)

Simple Roast Chicken (page 114)

Matzo Balls (page 29 or 30)

Chicken Broth (page 27 or 28)

Braised Purple Cabbage (page 148)

Hamantaschen (page 179)

It is customary on Purim to eat Hamantaschen, which are supposed to represent the crown of the evil King Haman.

Purim is among the "happiest" of the Jewish holidays, which makes it different from some of the serious ones like Yom Kippur.

It is so lighthearted, in fact, that the Jewish people are traditionally ordered to drink copious amounts of alcohol, so that they may not even remember the "bad guy"—King Haman.

On Purim it is customary to give alms, despite being wealthy or poor.

Very religious Jewish children do not typically observe Halloween, but on Purim they dress up in costumes and carry "graggers" or noisemakers and loudly boo the King as they walk around.

Make–Ahead Tips For Purim

2–3 Days Before	The Day Before	The Morning Of	2 Hours Before Eating	Shortly Before Eating
Make the Everything Crackers. (Store in an air-tight container.)	Make the Chopped Liver.	Bake the Challah.	Roast the chicken.	Reheat the cabbage.
Make the Braised Purple Cabbage.	Make the Hamantaschen.	Make the Matzo Ball dough.		Boil the matzo balls.
Make the Chicken Broth.				Heat the chicken broth for the soup.

Passover

Passover Menu

Matzo (page 44 or 47)

Charoset (page 219)

Salmon Gefilte Fish (page 23)

Fresh Horseradish Beet Sauce (page 223)

Matzo Ball (page 29 or 30)

Chicken Broth (page 27 or 28)

**Lemon-Coriander Grilled Lamb Chops
(page 126)**

Honey Dijon Asparagus (page 175)

**Raspberry Chocolate or Creamsicle
Macaroons (page 199 or 200)**

Chocolate-Covered Matzo (page 184)

Passover is celebrated in the spring of each year and is the oldest Jewish festival that has been observed continuously.

Passover is observed by hosting a Seder, which is a dinner and ceremony consisting of symbolic foods and prayers.

Matzo, or unleavened bread, is eaten during Passover. This is to remind us that there was no time for bread to rise as the flight from Egypt took place.

Children play an important role in the Passover Seder, making it a serious, yet entertainingly educational holiday.

For the duration of Passover, leavened foods are not allowed, making matzo ball soup and macaroons are favorite options, along with proteins and veggies, of course!

Make-Ahead Tips For Passover

2–3 Days Before	The Day Before	The Morning Of	Shortly Before Eating
Make the Horseradish Beet Sauce.	Make the Matzo and Chocolate-Covered Matzo.	Make the Charoset.	Grill the lamb chops.
Make the Chicken Broth. (Save a bone for the Seder plate!)	Make the Salmon Gefilte Fish. (Store with broth and carrots.)	Make the macaroons.	Boil the matzo balls.
Make the vinaigrette for the asparagus.	Marinate the lamb chops.	Make the matzo ball dough.	Roast the asparagus.
			Heat up the broth/soup.

Sukkot

Sukkot Menu

Simple Roast Chicken (page 114)

Sweet Potato Kugel (page 159)

Israeli Salad (page 164)

Rugelach (page 180)

Pita Bread (page 48)

Roasted Squash Hummus (page 19)

Baba Ghanoush (page 16)

Halvah (page 191)

There are two primary symbols of Sukkot, the lulav (palm leaf) and the etrog (or citron).

The lulav represents the backbone and the etrog represents the heart of the people.

Sukkot celebrates the escape of the Jewish people out of Egypt and during this holiday, we build outside structures with palm leaves and willow branches.

This structure is meant to represent that during the flight from Egypt temporary shelters had to be set up along the way.

During Sukkot all the meals are eaten under this structure, the Sukkah, so they must transport well and not be apt to spoiling.

Make-Ahead Tips For Sukkot

The Day Before	The Day Of
Make the Sweet Potato Kugel.	Make the pita.
Make the Rugelach.	Make the Israeli Salad.
Make the Halvah.	Make the roast chicken.
Make the Baba Ghanoush.	
Make the hummus.	

Rosh Hashanah

Rosh Hashanah Menu

Challah (page 52)

Tzimmes (page 151)

**Field Greens with Pomegranate Seeds
and Maple Vinaigrette (page 147)**

Bubbe's Brisket (page 117)

Sweet Potato Kugel (page 159)

Apple Kugel (page 187)

Honey Cake (page 192)

Rosh Hashanah is the Jewish New Year. Just like the New Year we celebrate by the lunar calendar, it is a mark of new beginnings.

A ram's horn, called a shofar, is blown each year, which makes quite a loud and impressive sound. It does not sound musical at all, and yet takes quite the skill level to execute.

Apples and honey are almost always eaten for this holiday. The idea is that you should celebrate with sweets for a sweet new year.

Challah is a bread which is served on every Sabbath (or Shabbat) year-round, but for Rosh Hashanah, it is sometimes served in round loaves to represent the circular nature of the year and the life span.

It is also customary to eat pomegranate seeds, not only because they are sweet, but also in the hopes that the New Year will be as full of good deeds as the pomegranate is of seeds.

Make-Ahead Tips For Rosh Hashanah

2–3 Days Before	The Day Before	The Morning Of	Shortly Before Eating
Make the brisket and slice, *returning to sauce or braising liquid.*	Make the Apple Kugel.	Make the Honey Cake.	Reheat the brisket; *remove from the refrigerator 1 hour before reheating, and then warm in a 300°F (150°C) oven for 45 minutes to 1 hour.*
Make the Tzimmes.	Make the Sweet Potato Kugel.	Make the Challah.	Reheat Tzimmes; *300°F (150°C) for 30 minutes.*
			Reheat kugels. (*Optional. Can be served at room temperature.*)

Yom Kippur

Yom Kippur Menu
(Breaking the Fast)

Bagels (page 56, 59 or 60)

Cashew Cream Cheese (page 231)

Smoked Whitefish Salad (page 89)

Traditional Egg Salad (page 109)

Sliced cucumber, tomatoes, red onions
and capers, for serving

Yom Kippur is the Day of Atonement (or forgiveness) in which Jewish people pray for forgiveness for the entire preceding year.

On this day there is a twenty-four-hour fast where the focus is on being forgiven and Jewish people typically stay in the synagogue all day.

However, at the end of the Day of Atonement and prayer, the fast is broken, often with a simple menu of egg salad, tuna salad, whitefish salad and bagels.

This is the most serious of the holidays and often the one that is observed the most out of all the others.

Make-Ahead Tips For Yom Kippur

3 Days Before	1 Day Before (Before Sundown)	The Day of , Shortly After Sundown, Before Breaking the Fast
Make the cream cheese.	Make the Smoked Whitefish Salad.	Slice cucumbers, tomatoes and red onion and arrange on a platter with capers to be served with the bagels and salads. Throw and toast bagels.
	Make the Traditional Egg Salad.	
	Make the Bagels. (*Freeze until ready to eat.*)	

Hanukkah

Hanukkah is observed by lighting candles each night. Each one is representative of the oil which miraculously kept burning for eight nights, despite there being only enough for one night.

The word Hanukkah translates to "Rededication."

Dreidel is a spinning top and a game that is played during Hanukkah with chocolate money or "gelt."

The four Hebrew letters represented on the sides of the dreidel are representative of the following phrase: "A great miracle happened there."

Candles are added each night, from right to left, because that is the same direction Hebrew is read. But the candles are actually lit from left to right as a sign of respect paid to the newer candles.

The reason that fried foods are the official Hanukkah fare is to celebrate the oil that miraculously lasted eight days instead of one.

Hanukkah dates do not, in fact, change every year. Hanukkah always begins on the 25th of the Jewish month of Kislev. However, since the Jewish calendar is lunar-based, rather than solar-based, where the 25th of Kislev falls on the secular, solar-based calendar changes from year to year.

Make-Ahead Tips For Hanukkah

2–3 Days Before	The Day Of	Shortly Before Eating
Make the short ribs.	Make the Latkes.	Assemble the salad
Make the maple vinaigrette.	Make the Sweet Potato Latkes.	Reheat the short ribs. *Remove from the refrigerator 1 hour before reheating, and then warm in the oven at 300°F (150°C) for 45 minutes to 1 hour.*
Make the gelt.		
Make the Applesauce.	*(Alternatively, these can both be made the day before if you're cooking for a crowd! Just store them in the fridge and reheat at 450°F (232°C) for 5–7 minutes in a single layer on a baking sheet.)*	Reheat latkes if you made them ahead of time.
Make the sour cream.		

Yiddish Glossary

So here's the thing; you don't have to know Yiddish to have a Yiddish Kitchen, but word on the street is if you can pronounce CHUTZPAH with the proper guttural "CH", your matzo balls can fool even the most frum bubbe and her tribe. Need help with your pronunciation? Just clear your throat of the residual bagel and lox you just ate, and you are well on your way. Now you are ready to conquer Jewish cooking like the maven you were born to be.

Baleboste: A good homemaker, a woman who's in charge of her home and will make sure you remember it. Ex. She's the kind of baleboste who makes grain-free bagels from Yiddish Kitchen.

Bisl: Or bissel—a little bit. Ex. I need a bisl of food to tide me over, before I plotz.

Bubbe: Or bobe. It means grandmother. Ex. My bubbe's matzo ball soup will leave you dreaming about it for days!

Bubula: An endearing term used for grandchildren or friends.

Chazer: Pig or slob. Ex. Can you believe how much babka Morty ate? What a chazer!

Chutzpah: Nerve, extreme arrogance, brazen presumption. In English, chutzpah often connotes courage or confidence, but, among Yiddish speakers, it is not a compliment. Ex. What chutzpah those two had to make matzo without wheat flour!

Dreck: Trash, rubbish. Ex. You think I should eat this garbage?! This is dreck—I'll stick with the recipes from *The New Yiddish Kitchen*.

Frum: Religiously observant. Ex. You know that Esther, if he was more frum he'd be seen at shul on more than just Yom Kippur!

Geshmak: Delicious, tasty or delightful if referring to a person Ex. All of the recipes I've made from *The New Yiddish Kitchen* have been geshmak!

Glitch: Or glitsh. Literally slip, skate or nosedive. Ex. There was a glitch in the system but good ol' Moishe ironed it out!

Goy: A non-Jew, a Gentile. As in Hebrew, one Gentile is a goy, many Gentiles are goyim. The non-Jewish world in general is "the goyim." Ex. Think Yiddish Kitchen is just for the Jews?! Nonsense! Even the goyim love it!

Klutz: Or better yet, klots. Literally means "a block of wood," so it's often used for a dense, clumsy or awkward person. Ex. Pick up your feet, you klutz!

Kosher: Something that's acceptable to Orthodox Jews, especially food. Ex. Did you see Chaya leaning into that man at the market? That's sure not kosher!

Kvetch: In popular English, kvetch means complain, whine or fret. Ex. Quit your kvetching and do something about it already!

Maven: Pronounced meyven. An expert, often used sarcastically. Ex. A real maven that one is—knows everything about everything!

Mazel Tov: Literally good luck (well, literally, good constellation), but it's a congratulation for what just happened, not a hopeful wish for what might happen in the future. Ex. Mazel tov, Gitl, many wishes for a bright future together!

Mentsh: An honorable, decent person, an authentic person, a person who helps you when you need help. Can be a man, woman or child. Ex. What a mentsh, that guy, donating his time and money for anyone in need!

Meshuga: Insanity or craziness. Ex: You must be meshuga if you think I am gonna stand for that!

Mishpocheh: Or mishpokhe or mishpucha. Family. Ex. The whole mishpocheh will be there, better prepare yourself!

Nosh: To nibble a light snack. Ex. I just need to nosh on something so I don't plotz!

Oy Gevalt: An expression conveying dismay or like "oh how awful." Ex. Oy gevalt, are you kidding me?! He is way too young for a girlfriend!

Oy Vey: Exclamation of dismay, grief or exasperation. Ex. Oy vey, did you see her skirt? If it got any shorter I could see her collar bones!

Plotz: Literally, to explode, as in aggravation. Ex. Don't plotz! I've got another batch of latkes coming out of the oil in just a minute!

Schlock: Cheap, shoddy, or inferior Ex. What a schlocky gift! The arms fell off of that doll before the wrapping paper came off.

Schmaltzy: Excessively sentimental, gushing, flattering, over-the-top, corny. From shmaltz, which means chicken fat or grease. Ex. That love story was cute I guess, but really a little too schmaltzy for my taste!

Schmooze: Chat, make small talk, converse about nothing in particular. Ex. You wanna get that job? Better start schmoozing now!

Schmuck: A derogatory term for a foolish or contemptible person, but you shouldn't use it in polite company, since it refers to male anatomy. Ex. After all she does for him, he forgot their anniversary. What a schmuck!

Schvitz: To sweat. Ex. Oy gevalt, this humidity! I'm schvitzing like a chazer!

Shalom: A greeting that means "deep peace." Ex. Shalom, my friend, I hope you are doing well.

Shayna Punim: Pretty face. Ex. She's not just another shayna punim, that one's got class and smarts too!

Shikse: A non-Jewish woman, all too often used derogatorily. Ex. Can you believe he married that shikse? Let's see how long THAT lasts.

Shlemiel: A clumsy, inept person, similar to a klutz (also a Yiddish word). Ex. That schlemiel couldn't fox-trot to save his life!

Shlep: To drag, traditionally something you don't really need; to carry unwillingly. Ex. You better pack a light bag, because I am not gonna be the one to shlep it from here to tomorrow!

Shlimazel: Someone with constant bad luck. Ex. That poor shlimazel can't seem to catch a break!

Shmutz: Or shmuts. Dirt—a little dirt, not serious grime. Ex. You got a little schmutz on your dress, go clean that up!

Shtick: Something you're known for doing, an entertainer's routine, an actor's bit, stage business; a gimmick often done to draw attention to yourself. Ex. His humor is sort of offensive but that's his schtick!

Spiel: A long, involved sales pitch. Ex. Oy, if I had to listen to much more of that spiel I was gonna kick him in the shins!

Tchotchke: Knick-knack, little toy, collectible or giftware. Ex. If she buys one more tchotchke, I am gonna schlep them to the dumpster!

Tsuris: Serious troubles, not minor annoyances. Ex. Like the plagues of Passover, now, those were tsuris!!!

Tuches: Rear end, bottom, backside, buttocks. Ex. Oy vey! What a pain in the tuches that one is!

Yenta: Female busybody or gossip. At one time, high-class parents gave this name to their girls (after all, it has the same root as "gentle"), but it gained the Yiddish meaning of "she-devil." Ex. Don't be such a yenta, mind your own business!

Yiddisher Kop: Smart person. Literally means "Jewish head." Ex. Be a yiddisher kop and make a batch of blintzes already!

Resources

If you are new to a grain- and dairy-free lifestyle, you may see some ingredients within these pages that are unfamiliar. Perhaps you've passed by these very items on your local grocery store shelves and never paid much attention, or perhaps you've never even heard of them before. This guide will help you familiarize yourself with some of our basic grain, dairy and refined sugar replacements, which we consider to be staples in our own homes. You can find more information and which brands we love most by visiting our online resource page at www.yiddishkitchen.com/resources.

Almond Flour: Finely milled almond flour is one of the more versatile grain-free flours used in grain- and gluten-free baking. It has an easy-to-work-with texture and can be used for baking, thickening, binding and even pasta making. Almond flour is carried in most health food stores and is now often found in the health foods section of your mainstream grocery. Most recipes in this book work best with blanced, finely ground almond flour.

Arrowroot Starch: Similar to tapioca in texture, arrowroot is a starch derived from the arrowroot plant and is easily digestible for those with food sensitivities. It is often used in baking, thickening and breading grain-free recipes. Arrowroot can typically be found in most health food stores and is now often found in the health foods section of your mainstream grocery.

Avocado Oil: This oil is fantastic for high-temperature cooking including baking, frying and sautéing. We prefer the oils mentioned here because they are higher in quality than most mainstream oils, which can often be rancid and unstable for higher cooking temperatures. It can typically be found in most health food stores and is now often found in the health foods section of your mainstream grocery.

Cassava Flour: This flour is the closest to regular wheat-based flour and is made from cassava or yuca root. This flour can occasionally be found in international markets, but the consistency and quality can be questionable. We prefer to buy ours online.

Chestnut Flour: Chestnut flour is made from dried, ground chestnuts. It is slightly sweet in flavor and a great grain-free alternative for baking or even making noodles. Chestnut flour can be found in Italian specialty stores or online.

Coconut Flour: Coconut flour is made from ground coconut meat and is a great nut-free alternative to other nut-based flours. It tends to be more "thirsty" than other grain-free flours, so less is needed in most recipes in order to prevent a dense end product. Coconut flour can typically be found in most health food stores and is now often found in the health foods section of your mainstream grocery.

Coconut Oil: This oil is also great for cooking high temperatures at like avocado oil, and is now more and more common in mainstream grocery stores. We prefer the oils mentioned here because they are higher in quality than most mainstream oils, which can often be rancid and unstable for higher cooking temperatures. It can typically be found in most health food stores.

Coconut Palm Sugar: Coconut sugar is derived from the sap of cut flower buds of the coconut palm. It is less refined than white sugar and tends to retain more of the fiber and nutrients, though it should still be used sparingly. Coconut sugar can typically be found in most health food stores and is now often found in the health foods section of your mainstream grocery.

Maple Sugar: Maple sugar is prepared from the sap of a maple tree. It has a higher glycemic index than coconut sugar, but makes a great alternative to refined white sugar. Maple sugar can typically be found in most health food stores and is now often found in the health foods section of your mainstream grocery.

Olive Oil: Olive oil is an easily attainable higher quality cooking oil, which does not become denatured in the cooking process like some cooking oils. It can be found in most mainstream grocery stores.

Palm Shortening: Palm shortening is a great substitute for butter as long as it's non-hydrogenated and substainably harvested.

Tapioca Starch: Tapioca is an easy-to-digest starch sourced from the yuca/cassava root. It is used in a similar manner as arrowroot in grain-free eating. While this starch comes from the same source as cassava flour, it has very different properties in cooking. Tapioca can often be substituted for arrowroot, but rarely can be substituted for cassava flour. Tapioca starch can typically be found in most health food stores and is now often found in the health foods section of your mainstream grocery. It can also be found in international markets, relatively inexpensively.

A Sheynem Dank (Thank You)

To our bubbes, for creating memories so lasting they became the impetus for this book; and for showing us the true definitions of chutzpah and strength.

To our parents, for collectively giving birth to us so that we could go on to re-create awesome Jewish recipes together and offer them to the world.

To our husbands, for eating all those carbs without kvetching or gaining weight. Actually, we aren't so happy about that second part—more like jealous.

To our offspring, both furry and human, for allowing us breaks from walking you, feeding you and cleaning up your poop, so that we could collaborate on this project and forever change the world, one latke at a time.

To all of our readers, Jews and goys alike, for helping us realize how much the universe was missing these allergen-friendly recipes; also for posting all of the best emojis when we post bagel photos.

And a big thanks to Page Street Publishing for channeling their inner Shalom and believing that the world is a better place with more bagels.

About the Authors

Simone Miller is a self-taught chef who has been in the culinary world for a decade and a half. She is the chef and owner of Zenbelly Catering, a 100% gluten-free catering company that specializes in Paleo cuisine and the author of *The Zenbelly Cookbook: An Epicurean's Guide to Paleo Cuisine.* Passionate about health and nutrition, Simone has made it her mission to show the world that Paleo fare can be just as elegant, delicious and artfully prepared as what you'd find in a fine bistro. She believes that when the focus is on quality, fresh ingredients, there is nothing restrictive about this way of life. After cooking all day in the catering kitchen, Simone truly values meals that can be made at home in a flash. She has been sharing her favorite recipes on her blog, *zenbelly.com.* There, Simone's focus is on demonstrating just how simple and beautiful eating well can be.

Jennifer Robins is the voice and whole-foodist behind the popular food blog *Predominantly Paleo,* and author of the bestselling book *Down South Paleo.* After being diagnosed with several autoimmune conditions and chronic infections, including Lyme disease, Jennifer became gravely ill and mostly housebound. When traditional medical treatments failed to help, Jennifer turned to food for healing. Removing grain, dairy and refined sugars and eating "predominantly Paleo," she started reclaiming her life, one whole-food at a time. As a wife and mother of three, Jennifer hopes to instill healthy habits in her children now in hopes of creating wellness for a lifetime.

Index